# No Second Place Winner

# No Second Place Winner

### by WILLIAM H. "BILL" JORDAN

Assistant Chief Patrol Inspector
U. S. Border Patrol

Seventeenth Printing 2006

Library of Congress Catalog Card Number: 65–22080

Photographs by Louis M. Werne, Jr.

Printed in the United States of America

Police Bookshelf
P.O. Box 122
Concord, NH 03302-0122
603-224-6814
ISBN 0-936279-09-5

# Dedication

OVER THE past thirty years I have been privileged to know and work with a group of men unique in the annals of law enforcement—the Peace Officers of our great Southwest. The word "group" is descriptive, for although they were of no one service they formed a close knit brotherhood, representative of all branches of government: state troopers and Texas Rangers, city police and village constables, sheriffs and their deputies, alcohol tax investigators, agents of the FBI and of the Treasury Department, and inspectors of the U. S. Border Patrol. Here the dissimilarity ended. They were cast from the same mold. To them, my compañeros of many years and many trails, this book is dedicated. It is written of the weapons and leather of which their lives were compounded and of the gun skills they learned in the smoke of little fights, important only to those involved. The highest praise that could be spoken by one of this group was to say, "He'll do to ride the river with." Thus I salute them, one and all. The world will not see their like again.

# Introduction

BILL JORDAN is the fastest man on the draw that I have ever seen in action. He has been practicing the quick draw for thirty years that I know of. You can get pretty sharp at slapping leather after three decades of practice. Bill can hold a ping pong ball on top of his hand, bare inches above the holstered gun, suddenly drop the ball, go for his shooting iron and blast the ball as it falls past the holster. You've got to be fast to do that.

What maybe makes more of an impression on me than his lightning draw is his point shooting accuracy. As a regular feature of a shooting exhibition he draws, shoots from the hip double action, and hits aspirin pills neatly lined up on a table some ten feet in front of him. And, if this was not enough, he winds up the amazing exhibition by splitting a playing card edgeways! Most fellows could not hit these tiny targets if they took deliberate aim and squeezed the trigger! Jordan says he can "feel" the gun point at these peewee targets. It appears to the slightly goggle-eyed onlooker that his .357 must have built-in radar! When, in addition to the above, you consider that this man is an NRA Lifetime Master with the pistol, big bore rifle and small bore rifle; a "AA" skeet and trap-shooter; and a Distinguished Marksman; it becomes apparent that when he speaks about shooting it will be worth while to listen.

Although most of his time is occupied by his duties as Assistant Chief Patrol Inspector with the United States Border Patrol, Bill is much in demand and appears often as a public relations gesture for his Service at civic and social clubs and as an instructor at police academies around the country.

For the past seven consecutive years he has instructed classes in fast draw and combat shooting in the police section of the Small Arms Firing School at the National Pistol Matches. He uses his leave touring the country putting on quick draw and fast shooting exhibitions on the circuit of the Knife and Fork Clubs, Inc. Looking the typical Texan, at least six and-a-half feet tall and as lanky as a beef critter eating greasewood, Jordan has a repertoire which fits his appearance and his shooting. He never resorts to any "trick" shooting. Everything is on the up-and-up and all his demonstration is entirely practical with safety stressed throughout. The equipment used is the working rig of officers all over the country, a Sam Browne belt with holster of his design and a .357 double action revolver. He fires wax bullets when performing indoors.

With thirty years as a federal officer behind him, Jordan has a rich background for the authorship of this treatise on gun fighting. He has rubbed shoulders with gun fighters throughout the years; talked to scores of them; compared notes and watched them in practice. These associations, together with his own three decades of law enforcement, place him in the unique position of probably being our best authority on a game in which, as he so aptly puts it, there are "no second place winners."

I commend this book to you as the best thing I have read on a highly fascinating subject.

*Colonel Charles Askins*

# Table of Contents

CHAPTER ONE . . . . . . . . . . . . 11

FIGHTIN' LEATHER . . . . . . . . . . . 19

CARE AND FITTING OF HOLSTER . . . . . . . 35

GRIPS . . . . . . . . . . . . . 39

FAST DRAW . . . . . . . . . . . . 45

SIDEARMS . . . . . . . . . . . . 67

CALIBERS AND LOADS . . . . . . . . . . 75

PRACTICE LOADS . . . . . . . . . . . 83

COMBAT STYLE SHOOTING . . . . . . . . . 91

GUN FIGHTING . . . . . . . . . . . 101

SUMMATION . . . . . . . . . . . . 113

# Chapter One

THE BORDER between two countries has always had a powerful attraction for the lawless of both. It offers two advantages to such characters by its very nature. First, the lure of a quick buck to be picked up by smuggling into and out of both countries. Second, the convenience of getting a running start away from retribution by crossing over to temporary sanctuary in the adjacent country. It is a natural consequence that armed clashes between criminals and officers are more common in such areas than elsewhere. Along our Mexican border the frequency of these affrays reached epic proportions during the days of national prohibition and the great depression. That they are less frequent today is the sum of several factors: repeal of prohibition; national prosperity; good roads into isolated areas; and the lesson painfully learned by the border characters that they invariably came out on the short end when they attempted armed resistance. This lesson was patiently taught over and over again by a hardbitten brotherhood of instructors, the peace officers of our great Southwest. The Border Patrol was a member in good standing of that distinguished faculty.

Before these lessons were fully absorbed by the smuggling gentry, gunfights along the Rio Grande became so commonplace that officers not involved seldom bothered to investigate the shooting. They just assumed that another class was in session and went about their affairs in confidence that the lesson plan would be followed faithfully, efficiently, and with all deliberate speed.

As could be expected with such experienced fighters involved, many of these battles ended with the case marked closed and no further legal action necessary, other than that required of the nearest coroner.

It will be evident in the following chapters that this book has not been written with the entertainment of the reader as a primary goal. It is more in the nature of a text dealing with entirely serious aspects of an area of gun usage little covered by other writings with which I am familiar. However, as any good officer can tell you, law enforcement is not entirely the humorless profession it must appear to the outside observer. Mostly, the few anecdotes which will be used herein fit in with the text material and are included to illustrate or drive home some point. So perhaps in this opening chapter, with no attempt at correlation with any point made in the book, a few observations and stories illustrating that these affairs are occasionally leavened by a humorous or even comic touch will not be amiss. While apropos to nothing else herein they may serve to lighten what is otherwise admittedly a grim business. Actually, since in review the above reasoning seems a little lame, I may as well admit that my publisher advised me confidentially that, strictly from a commercial viewpoint, he considered the book to be a little on the thin side . . . and suggested that I add a little filler material to fatten it up . . . like a few wild stories of perilous adventures and derring do . . . thus making it appear more attractive to the buying public, and giving them a feeling of having gotten their money's worth through sheer weight of material.

Now, I have found that adventures are usually the result of inefficiency or lack of planning and can be best defined as something you didn't realize you had until you were safe back at home where you were wishing you were when you were having it. Nevertheless, while not wishing to clutter up the remainder of the book, at the same time I am not one to argue with a publisher or to let brevity interfere with prosperity. Which accounts for my now being in the unusual position of writing this first chapter after having finished the book. —Oh, well. . . .

There was the night in El Paso when a Border Patrol team, going in to the river at dusk to watch a hot crossing, ran head on into a smuggling train coming out of the river at that point. Now these affairs had been going on so long that they had through custom become pretty highly formalized. The boss smuggler would hire *Pistoleros* to guard his shipment, the number and quality of these reflected in the value of the cargo and the prestige to be maintained or enhanced by the smuggler. These *Pistoleros,* with the highest paid and most *valiente* leading the way, formed the vanguard. The "bearers" followed them with some of the lesser bravos and the smuggler himself bringing up the rear. Generally speaking, polite usage required that certain amenities be observed before hostilities were opened. One of the Patrol group was expected to sing out *Manos Arriba. Federales!*—meaning, "Hands up. Federal Officers!" At this challenge the smugglers had several avenues open to them. They could follow instructions; drop everything and run; or fight; all according to the mood of the moment, the tactical situation, and/or the quality of the escort. On this particular occasion the surprise of the meeting was so complete that someone impolitely fired a shot without waiting for the conventional challenge and instantly the shooting became general. Most of the smugglers, after dropping the contraband, got safely back across the river. Normally at this point they would have been expected to shrug the whole thing off as one of the vicissitudes of the business in which they were engaged and with true Latin philosophy conclude that it hadn't been such a good idea for today to begin with—so—maybe next week things would be better.

But this was different! Filled with indignation at what must have been considered a complete failure to observe the proper amenities, as soon as their own side of the river was reached, a hot fire was opened on the side they had just departed. Of course, the Border Patrolmen were likewise outraged at this open display of bad manners. And since it also appeared probable that some violation of International Law was involved by this unwarranted aggression on the part of their opponents—like possibly lack of proper respect for U. S. territory—after due consideration, the fire was returned. Friends of the combatants on the Mexican side heard the commotion and hastened to the aid of their embattled compatriots. Likewise, all Border Patrolmen, and in fact apparently everyone else within earshot, joined in and the battle became general. So general that on *this* side of the river people that *nobody* knew were coming up to the officers and borrowing ammunition!

Everybody was having a good time—it beat sitting and watching a dull crossing where nothing was happening—and nobody was getting hurt to amount to anything, so the battle raged all night until daylight brought its reminders of responsibilities and the fight was mutually brought to a halt.

These responsibilities were quickly brought to the attention of the Senior Border Patrol officer on the scene when he received "the word" that the District Director wished to "confer" with him about the evening's activities. He approached this interview with considerable misgiving, and rightly so, the District Director being an irascible old gentleman by the name of Mr. Wilmoth who was noted for eating Patrol officers without bothering to slick down their ears; and who was further known to take the dimmest of views of such carryings on as had occurred during the late evening's festivities—regrettably, but undeniably, under the supervision of this aforementioned young Senior.

Upon entering the Director's "den" his worst fears were quickly realized. He was met with a roar that blasted him back on his heels and which translated into something like "I want an explanation as to why once that smuggling train was back across the river you didn't take your men and get to work instead of fooling around there enjoying yourselves all evening like you did?"

With admirable presence of mind under the circumstances the young officer countered hopefully with, "Mr. Wilmoth, I wanted to leave there the worst

**13**

way! But the fire from the other side was so intense that we were hopelessly pinned down. Why, it was all a man's life was worth just to lift his head—much less try to leave!"

I think it best to pull the curtain at this point. You see, Mr. Wilmoth was aware of the three details which had gone back to headquarters during the night to bring up more ammunition!

Just last week my attention was rudely directed to how much thought can be colored by a difference of viewpoint. In the foregoing account I have spoken of Mr. Wilmoth, a man whom I admired very much, as "an irascible old gentleman." Actually, I had no real idea of how old he was at the time. I suppose I thought of him as being somewhere in his late nineties. Thinking back I suspect that early fifties would have been about right. Be that as it may be, my initiation into the other side of this youthful viewpoint came about through a surprise inspection that I pulled on a group of Border Patrol Trainees. These young men, who were undergoing their rigid one year's training and probation, were reporting for shift duty and their presence idling around the office suggested to my mind the probability that an inspection of their sidearms would be good for their general development as officers. Particularly if I found any of the weapons in need of attention.

To make a very thorough inspection short, those guns were all in beautiful condition. Immaculate! However, having gone that far it would not have argued well for constituted authority in general and my "face" in particular, if I had found them so, officially. Nor would it have improved their future attention to pertinent detail. Accordingly, under very close scrutiny into such obscure spots as the narrow space between the top strap and the end of the barrel, I was able to find a bit of lint here and a speck of dried grease there. . . . After giving them about fifteen minutes of fatherly comments on the virtue of industry and the importance of having their artillery in perfect condition, I ended with, "Now you go get those guns CLEAN and don't ever let me see them in such a deplorable condition again."

A short time later I had occasion to go by the small room where cleaning equipment was kept. All were there industriously engaged in shining up the already glistening hardware. As I came abreast of the door, one of the boys whose back was toward me, held his revolver up, squinted judiciously into its insides and voiced the following opinion: "Well, I'll tell you one thing. The old --- -- - ----- can SEE!"

As the curtain was pulled for me so many years before, so, mercifully, do I drop it now!

**14**

Although the offenders along our borders are not quite such forthright characters as they were a few years back, human nature has changed but little. They have learned that discretion is the better part of valor, but criminals today have one thing in common with their counterparts of the past. They still resent being arrested and this resentment is the basis of an occasional violent episode even today. These are fortunately few and far between and some of our spirited young Border Patrol officers, never having experienced a gunfight, long for the excitement and thrills the old timers tell such fascinating lies about. All of which makes it the more memorable when these young fellows do get the chance to play gun fighter, as happened a few months ago at El Paso. Possibly you will remember reading about it in the papers. A man and his son decided to hijack a jet plane. President Kennedy issued orders that the plane was not to be allowed to leave under any circumstances. The Border Patrol was sent out to keep it on the ground! There was broad newspaper and TV coverage showing Border Patrol cars chasing that big airplane, shooting the tires, with an occasional shot up through the wings and fuselage for good measure. That was the answer to a pistol toter's dream, and one must admit those young fellows did a good job of stopping the plane—Of course, credit should be given where credit is due. They didn't do all this without help. There were agents of the Federal Bureau of Investigation riding in those cars too.—How else can those wild shots be explained?

And speaking of "wild shots" (or to use a better descriptive word, "accidental" shots), which an officer was sometimes faced with the necessity of explaining, brings up the subject of "alibi guns." To the unitiated, a hypothetical case would doubtless explain this piece of equipment more clearly than any other method. Let us suppose that an officer is checking freight trains at night. He receives urgent information that a man had just shot and killed two policemen in the adjoining town and was believed to have caught and be riding the freight our officer is about to check. The killer is described as "medium height and weight, wearing a brown hat, khaki pants and shirt, believed to be heavily armed and of course, obviously dangerous." As the train pulls into the yard and stops, a man, answering that description in externals, steps from between two box cars. Anticipating the possibility of trouble, our officer has his gun in one hand and his flashlight in the other. Flashing the light on the suspect he says, "I am an officer. Don't move!" Then, instead of obeying the order, the suspect reaches for his hip pocket. What would YOU do? Well, so did our hypothetical officer! But, supposing further, when he goes over to examine the remains, he finds that it was all a mistake. This man wasn't armed. Instead,

**15**

he had a bad cold and had selected a particularly unfortunate time to decide he needed a handkerchief to blow his nose. Although completely sincere in his conviction that his life was in danger and despite the fact that HAD this been the man the officer believed him to be, his wife would in all probability by now be a widow if he had waited to see what came out of that hip pocket, our officer is in a bad spot. That's where the alibi gun came in. It was a small, inexpensive gun of the "Owl Head" or "Saturday Night Harrison" persuasion, was fully loaded and would shoot, had no fingerprints on it and all in all was a very comforting thing to have around for the "suspect" to hold until the coroner got there! If this looks like an unethical action to you, it is suggested that you go back and again put yourself in the officer's spot. Then do a little honest soul searching before adopting a "holier than thou" attitude.

Well, alibi guns are no longer needed and are a thing of the past, so I am told. But to get to the story this was all leading up to. Which had to do with a young Border Patrol officer who early one evening had shot a notorious smuggler when they met *"mano a mano"* in the middle of a bridge over a large irrigation canal. The inquest was being held, late that same evening, at the coroner's office. If this seems strange to you, perhaps some background explanation is in order. The coroner was newly elected, and upon taking office had proved extremely zealous in the performance of his duties. When informed that his predecessor had made a practice of holding inquests into all deaths of a violent nature in the safety of his office, he stated publicly that this was a sorry way to do business, as was only to be expected of his late opponent. However, while HE was in office all inquests would be held, as was proper, at the scene of the violence. This new policy lasted only one day. Upon stepping out on the bank of the Rio Grande to view a "scene" at close hand he had been fired on by a .30–30 from the other bank. Whereupon righteous resolutions went by the board. Which brings us back to the inquest in point—at the coroner's office.

In telling his story the Border Patrolman stated that he had halted the smuggler on the bridge whereupon that worthy had immediately fired three shots at him from a palmed pistol, but that his willingness to commit murder so far exceeded his skill that he missed with all three shots. The officer, recovering from his surprise, finally got off one shot which proved adequate, ending the affray and the career of the subject of the inquest. At this stage it was pointed out that no gun had been found on or near the deceased. By way of explanation the officer said, "Well, when I shot him, his gun flew out of his hand, hit on the bridge and bounced off into the canal." It was decided to recess until morning and then drag for the missing weapon.

**16**

Now, I knew this young man well, and I knew that he would not lie. Not to me, anyway, and he had told me exactly the same story that he had told the coroner. If he said the smuggler had shot at him three times before he returned the fire, I knew that this was true. However, I also knew that the canal over which the fight had taken place was very large and that a pistol was a proportionately small and hard to find object. Thinking of the implications I found that I could not get to sleep. Finally, I gave up trying and slipping a small revolver remarkably similar to the one described as a typical alibi gun into my shirt pocket, I drove out to the scene of the affray and leaned over the bridge railing trying to estimate where the lost gun would most likely be located. As I gazed down at the moonlit water I saw and heard a splash which prompted me to feel hastily at the shirt pocket where I had been carrying my gun. My concern was justified. It had fallen out into the water below.

I can only give a second hand report of the wrap up of the case since I somehow felt that it would be better if I took up some just remembered but urgent business instead of attending in person. At the continuation the following morning with the entire cast assembled at the bridge, a large, powerful magnet which had been acquired for the occasion was lowered into the water. As it was moved slowly back and forth across the bottom, tension began to build. Finally, just before the suspense became unbearable, it was pulled up and lowered to the bridge planking for inspection. There was a great sigh of relief, for there, firmly held to the magnet, was a gun. The case was immediately dismissed with the judgment that the officer had fired in self defense. In fact, one of the jurymen later told me privately and in strict confidence that it was the worst case of justifiable homicide he had ever seen . . . for in addition to the previously mentioned gun, there had been five more picked up by the magnet—all positively identified as having belonged to the deceased—and each with three shots fired!

Well, the book is thickened and I'll write no more; not even to please the publisher! You see, as I dug into memory for these stories it occurred to me that wordiness could be as expensive as brevity. Who knows? Someday I may want to write another book!

# Fightin' Leather

MANY INTERESTING methods for "toting" pistols have been devised by gentlemen not hampered by regulations or orthodox thinking, but motivated simply with an earnest desire to survive by getting the edge on outstanding local competition. Included in the most novel of these are John Wesley Hardin's famous gun vest; half-breed holsters which turned on a swivel, allowing the gun to be tilted up, without drawing, and fired through the open end of the holster; and among the most ingenious, simply a string running under the coat from the left hand, up the sleeve, across the shoulders and down the right sleeve to where a gun was concealed just within the cuff. Either by turning loose the string with the left hand or hunching the shoulders, the gun was dropped into the right palm ready for action. Our more modern designers have not been outdone by the old timers in outlandish inventions, as witness the Clam Shell and holsters designed to be worn in such intimate locations as to be available only by unzipping the trousers.

If these screwball innovations are given the consideration they merit and ignored, holsters can best be classified by the carrying position and fall into three types. These are: cross draw, hip draw, and shoulder holster.

The shoulder holster we can, to a large degree, omit from this discussion. Its greatest value is for plain clothes use and for carrying large, sometimes scope-sighted, guns on hunting trips. I have never found one which I could wear with comfort. It has another disadvantage: crossing the target—which will be discussed under the cross draws.

Uniformed police, almost without exception, carry their weapons in either cross draw holsters or hip holsters. The cross draw is a comfortable holster, very fast under ideal conditions but lacking the mobility of the draw from the right hip. Its greatest disadvantage is a natural result of its position. When drawn it is usually swinging *across* the target and must be stopped or fired within a narrow limitation for a hit—as opposed to a hip draw where the gun is swung up *through* the target and has about six feet in which it may be fired successfully. The cross draw position has been extolled as ideal for the officer who, alone, is conveying a prisoner or prisoners in an unsecured automobile. This is a dangerous practice but sometimes necessary. Needless to say, under

Jesse Thompson belt clip rig. You can't get much more elemental—or faster. Stud welded to gun frame fits in metal slot on belt. Allows gun to be tilted up and fired without "drawing" for all out close range speed or shoved forward out of slot where less speed but more accuracy is desirable. Demonstrated by Elmer Keith.

The cross draw holster is an invitation to disaster. Its position is even more convenient to an opponent than to the wearer.

Front view of the Berns-Martin holster. The southpaw wearing it is Col. Charles Askins, of whom Harlon Carter once remarked, "Carlos used to be real clever with that rig!"

no conditions should a prisoner be permitted in the back seat where the officer would be defenseless. From a position of the prisoner in the front seat alongside the officer the weapon would be in the worst possible position if worn on the right hip; however, on the left hip for a cross draw would also be far from ideal. Only slight pressure on the officer's right elbow by the prisoner would prevent the gun being drawn with that hand, or used if it could be reached. The logical place to carry a gun under the circumstances described is not in a holster. Thrust into the right front of the belt for a left-handed cross draw, the right elbow can be used to fight the assailant off while the left hand draws the gun and restores order to the front seat.

More and more departments have adopted the right hip position as standard. It is now overwhelmingly the most used gun carrying position for obvious reasons. For one, it looks more natural and consequently unobtrusive, an effect to be desired. Under surprise conditions and awkward body or hand positions, the draw from the right hip is least complicated and least likely to put the officer at a disadvantage. It is in a position where it can be readily protected by the strongest and most dexterous hand; and, as previously mentioned, the gun, when drawn, will usually come up through the long axis of the target, allowing more leeway for error and a surer hit.

Since the right hip carry is the most popular and most desirable position, some discussion of equipment available and how it should be worn is in order. The plain, open top style, in most general use, is generally conceded to be the most practical and efficient holster available and is the holster of which this chapter is most descriptive. In addition to it, two other holsters designed to be worn on the right hip are in some usage. One of these, a type in which the weapon is held in place by flat springs and is drawn by shoving it forward through the slitted front of the holster, is known as the Berns-Martin model. This holster has attained considerable well-merited popularity. Its strongest point is the security with which the weapon is carried. Due to the holster's construction the gun could not be taken from behind by an assailant and could only be pulled out through the front of the holster. It is at its best in locations where the officer must work in thick crowds. It is my opinion that its greatest drawbacks are that it does not expose enough of the gun butt or any of the trigger guard; it offers resistance in drawing followed by complete lack of resistance as the weapon is freed from the retaining springs, making control and alignment difficult; and last, possibly a minor point but one which has affected its popularity adversely, it is homely. Although not as fast and not

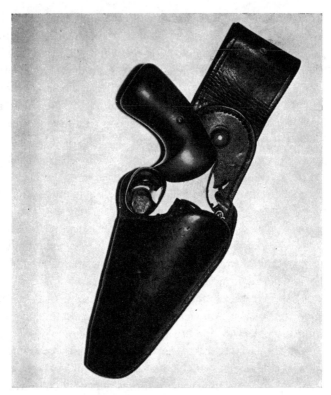

"Clamshell" holster, closed position.

allowing as positive control as the open type, this is a rugged, reliable holster which will give good service.

The second of the holsters mentioned above is the Clam Shell, of which perhaps the less said the better. It is operated by sticking a forefinger in the trigger guard and punching a concealed spring catch which causes the two sides of the holster to spring apart, usually leaving the gun in the user's hand. At one time this holster had a safety factor worth considering as the weapon cannot be drawn unless the location of the hidden spring is known. This advantage has been lost since hardly a criminal—or, as has been mischievously demonstrated—even a juvenile, today but knows the "secret" of where to poke a finger. Of course the serious faults of this holster are: the catches have been known to jam so that the officer was unable to get his gun out; they have sprung open "unpoked" allowing the gun to fall out on the ground; and they are even uglier than the Berns-Martin! Possibly the clearest commentary that can be

**24**

The "Clamshell" holster in open position. Halves fly apart when covered spring just forward of trigger in trigger guard is punched.

given is that use of the Clamshell holster, along with use of a cross draw or shoulder holster, is barred by the rules of the National Police Combat Matches, since all are considered dangerous.

As a first premise, we must conclude that any holster must be a compromise between speed and security. You can so secure the weapon that no one could remove it from the holster, not even the owner! On the other hand, a holster could be designed with only speed in mind to an extent that the gun falls out at the slightest movement. A happy medium between these two should be attained. A good safety strap, designed to fit either snapped over the hammer for security or snapped out of the way on the back of the holster when speed seems more important, can go far toward bridging the gap between these two extremes. It is my opinion that the full potential of this strap is not utilized in common practice. Most officers normally carry the weapon with the strap over the hammer, removing it only when they feel that quick action might be

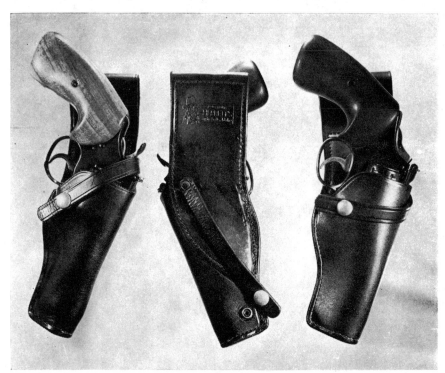

Safety strap should be designed to fit perfectly in either of three positions: Left, behind hammer or rear sight, giving complete security in the event strenuous action is necessary; Center, cleared for action. Capable of being snapped completely out of the way at back of holster; Right, snapped around front to allow easy access to gun and still "show off" a little polished brass.

imminent. This process should be reversed, and the gun snapped in only if strenuous action—running, crawling, climbing a boxcar, etc.,—is anticipated. In such cases there will always be time to secure the gun, whereas there might not be time for *un*-snapping if it was needed in a hurry. There is no way to draw a gun secured by a safety strap without running a risk of winding up with your fingers full of strap. Springs in the strap won't help if it is attached to the holster. It will still be a hazard. Spring models which allow the strap to "fly away" are also impractical for a working rig. They *can* become entangled with the fingers—and replacements are expensive. You would surely lose a lot of them at night. There is only one place for that strap: snapped completely out of the way on the back of the holster. One other argument against unsnapping for an emergency: Suppose you start walking toward a car you have stopped, unsnapping the safety strap as you go, and it turns out that the occupant is a prominent taxpayer? He is not going to like that "threatening" gesture and will probably register a complaint with your department, his congressman, and the local press.

Here then are the things that a holster should do: It should hold the gun securely yet allow the maximum speed attainable within the limits of comfort, safety, and security. To do this it must be designed to hold the gun in a perpendicular position and, viewed from the front, with the butt straight fore and aft, slanting neither in nor out; the whole weapon pointing straight at the ground with little or no deviation from the vertical. From a side view there should be a definite forward slant. This forward slant is for comfort only, to clear the gun butt and the toe of the holster from contact with the back of the seat when riding in a car. A great deal of mystery has been made of this "exact" tilt the holster should have. Exhaustive tests have shown there is no significant difference in speed, under realistic conditions, whether the holster be tilted forward or backward or hung straight up and down. There *is* a significant difference in comfort if you ride all day with your weapon being pushed forward by the car cushion. By the same token the drop should be just enough that the holster bottom is not pushed up by the seat. The amount of drop should be regulated by the length of "rise" of the individual officer. There has been much argument, written and oral, on this subject. As a practical matter it deserves no mention, since a low slung holster would look ridiculous on a law enforcement officer, he would be impeded in physical action, and could only be comfortable standing without motion. Accordingly, the only discussion which could be considered seriously justifiable would concern the purely academic question of whether a high or low holster position was best for sheer speed of draw. In various articles on the subject I have been cited as an example by authors advocating the high position. One such which comes to mind posed the question, "Why does Jordan use the high position?" and then went on to explain in some detail my reason. Actually, the reasons he gave were good. He pointed out the obvious advantages to an officer listed above and added that with the hand close to the weapon it would not have picked up much speed when contact was made with the gun; at which point it would be further slowed down by the weight of the weapon. Further away, as would be the case if the gun was worn higher, the hand would be traveling faster when the gun was encountered, plus the advantage of rocking the gun out already in shooting position instead of having to lift it into line from a low hung position. As a matter of fact, although I concur with all this reasoning, I would have given a much simpler reason for wearing my gun as I do had I been consulted before the article was written. I wear it there because Border Patrol regulations specify this position! And having become accustomed to feeling the comforting weight of a sixshooter in that same spot for many years I would be uneasy about trying to wear it somewhere else. It's like the stiff brim campaign

Five different angles of tilt, backward and forward, from the straight drop holster in center. No appreciable difference in speed could be detected after practice with each.

hats we wear as part of the dress uniform. If you get one that doesn't fit properly, that's bad, because it will never change; however, if you keep wearing it, in time your head will conform somewhat to the shape of the hat! The same is true of your gun. Regardless of where you wear it, pick one spot and stick with it until your hand will go to that spot instinctively.

The little experimenting I have done in this respect has been inconclusive. This is possibly because I have never used the low position enough to become accustomed to it. I have had a theory that a low position was a probable advantage for speed with a single action. This theory was borne out for a while in that winners of the single action fast draw matches for a long time wore such rigs; however, this has been completely reversed of recent years. High holsters, featuring excessive back slants and contoured to allow the gun to be drawn "sideways," have broken all past records and are used

**28**

almost exclusively by the high scoring fast draw competitors today.

Naturally, the holster should be so fashioned as to give easy access to the butt and trigger at the same time it protects the weapon and its sights. Once again a compromise. In this respect, the best description I can give of the desired effect is, "when you reach you just get a handful of gun."

Correct angle of tilt for officers holster clears butt of gun and toe of holster from back of car seat. Drop is correct if bottom of holster barely fails to touch seat.

In order to get out of a holster what was designed into it, a properly fitting belt, properly worn, is a must. The best holster design is worthless if worn on a belt that is too narrow for the holster loop or too soft to hold the holster in the position it was designed to assume. The belt should fit the holster loop tightly, be of good quality leather, firm, and worn snugly buckled straight across the body with no looseness or "cowboy slant." Such a slant gives a dashing, swashbuckling appearance which is only impressive to the inexperienced. It is the hallmark of the rookie cop. How many times have you noticed how much a part of the man is the gun on an experienced officer—or how often the rookie looks like a gun with man attached! Of course the reason, other than appear-

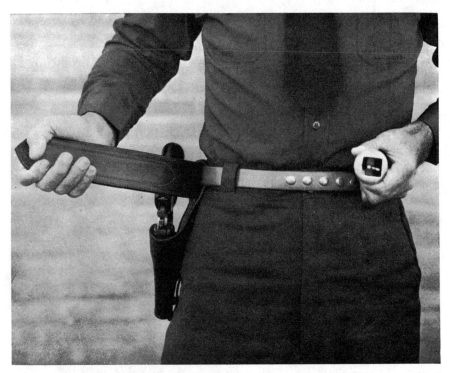

*Pants belt slipped through loop of holster to anchor it more solidly and prevent change of position.*

ance, that the belt should not be loosely slanted is that if the gun hangs even slightly, gun, holster, belt and all ride up and you've got a "handful of everything." None of which you can use for defense until the gun is separated from the rest of the confusion. If this should happen in a gunfight, your embarrassment would be short-lived!

The belt should not only be buckled snugly directly over the trouser belt, but a good trick is to also slip the trouser belt through the holster loop and cinch *it* down firmly before fastening the gun belt. This is made even more effective if you can get your wife to remove the trouser belt loops on the right side and reposition them so as to have one directly in front and one directly behind the holster when it is positioned to suit you. When the trouser belt is threaded under these loops and through the holster loop, no up or down movement of the gun belt or sliding of the holster is possible.

A desirable design feature is an enclosed strip of metal running from about

**30**

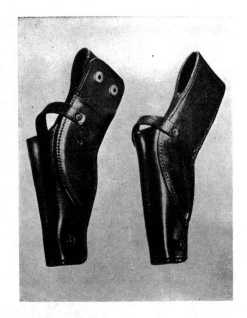

Holster on right has plain belt loop with metal extending to top of loop. One on left is "snap off" model with metal stopping at bottom of belt loop. Each has its advantages. For general "field" use the solid loop model is best. Holsters illustrated here and most of those shown in book were manufactured by Hume Leathergoods and by Herretts.

the middle of the back of the holster, through the shank, to the top of the belt loop. The metal should be slightly curved to fit the contour of the body and the cylinder of the revolver. This type should always be used, without a snap-off feature of the belt loop when a river belt or Sam Browne belt without shoulder strap or dees is uniform. With this construction, if the belt is snugly buckled, the gun and holster rides smoothly without movement or flapping, regardless of the violent action that might be required. It becomes literally part of the man, following his every movement.

For use where the Sam Browne, with dees, is uniform and the officer's duty is such that he is required to wear the belt without sidearm much of the time each day, a "snap-on" type is more convenient. There are disadvantages to this type holster. The metal can only be brought to the bottom of the belt loop, allowing the holster to "work" at this point, eventually wearing and becoming floppy. The second disadvantage, of course, is that snaps do not always stay snapped. If they should come loose from a motorcycle officer's belt while he was traveling at high speed, some marring of gun and holster could be expected. The type with solid loop and metal extending to top should be chosen by officers on field duty.

As previously mentioned, the length of this reinforced shank should be predicated on the build of the man. The officer of short stature who desires that

**31**

Officer with short "rise" who wishes to use holster with longer drop is compelled to go to swivel holster or be uncomfortable. Swivel should be locked except when officer is seated.

his gun be positioned lower is faced with two alternatives: be uncomfortable, or wear a swivel holster. If the latter is his choice, the drop should not be extreme; the swivel should be a type which can be positively locked in position; and should otherwise contain all the features mentioned above.

Holsters for plain clothes wear have the added requirement that they carry the gun inconspicuously. A shoulder holster fulfills this requirement, but is

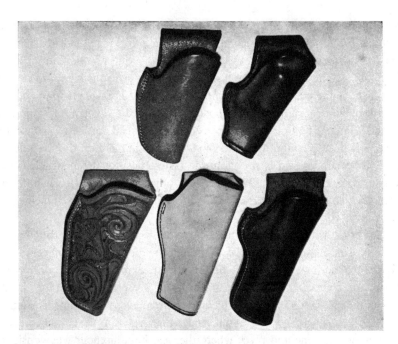

Above: Five good plain clothes holsters. All essentially the same type designed for wear on right hip. The holster in middle of bottom row has double belt loops which allow it to be worn on right hip or as cross draw. Below: The "Legace" holster for carrying a hideout gun strapped to the ankle.

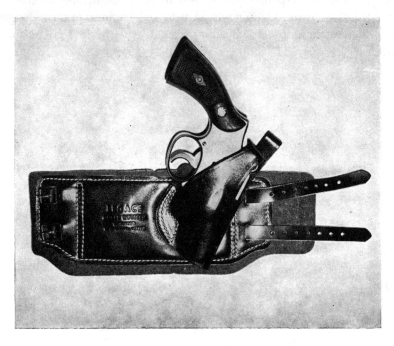

uncomfortable and subjects the gun to heavy doses of perspiration in a warm climate. Either a holster designed to make the gun ride behind the right hip or the cross draw type is most efficient, comfortable and practical in my opinion. It should ride high, and for the hip carry, directly over the right hip pocket. In fact, I shove the end of the holster into the pocket. This serves to anchor it and affords extra concealment if the coat tail should lift slightly for some reason. In this "far back" position some speed is sacrificed for better concealment. The cross draw position, with the gun worn well in front on the left side, offers good concealment and is probably the fastest position from which it can be drawn from under a coat. However, the objections offered elsewhere in this treatment concerning accuracy and the danger inherent in this method of carrying a gun apply.

This book has been written in the hope that things learned through trial and error over a long period of time might be of value to brother officers of lesser experience and not as a vehicle to advertise any product. Most of the comments contained herein are a voicing of my personal opinion, based on this experience. Others, and all of the requirements of equipment listed, have met the test of usage by myself and other veteran peace officers of the Southwest at a time and place where the best in equipment was considered a prime essential of survival. It would be strange indeed if the features of equipment, which I have listed as desirable, did not coincide closely with the features of belts and holsters of my design; since these designs are based on the thought, trial, and experience mentioned above. While making no claim that I have the only answer, I have no doubt as to the soundness of these designs and feel no hesitation in recommending them. "They'll do to ride the river with."

# Care and Fitting of Holster

THE BEST that can be bought can never be too good for the officer whose life may depend on the quality of his equipment. Design must be based on thought and trial, and the material and workmanship must be the best obtainable. It is the responsibility of every officer to himself, his family, his brother officers, and the public to see that this is true. But the responsibility does not end here. The finest examples of the leatherworkers' art can be ruined in short order by misuse, carelessness or misinformation.

A new holster, properly made, is always slightly undersized. This is because although cured leather can easily be stretched to a custom fit, it can be shrunk very little. Unless it has been preblocked by the maker, which can usually be ascertained by reading his literature or a visual examination of the holster, the gun should not be forced home until the leather has been softened by soaking. To do so will mar the leather and a perfect fit will never be attained.

If your holster is not preblocked, here's the way to go about it: throw it in the horse trough, or some other vessel of water, and let it soak for about two hours, until the leather feels soft. This will not harm the holster in any way. Shake off the excess water and wipe dry. Carefully insert revolver, which has been *lightly* oiled all over, inside and out. Be sure that the barrel centers the holster. This you can tell by noting that the ring left by the end of the barrel on the leather plug closing bottom of holster is centered. Work the leather with your fingers until it perfectly matches the contours of the gun. At this point the gun should be removed, wiped thoroughly dry, and re-oiled. Now put it back in the holster and let it dry overnight. A good trick at this stage is to line the holster with a small piece of the thin plastic bag cleaning companies use to protect clothing. If you do this, be sure that it is not bunched, which might spoil the contours of the holster. The next morning remove the gun (and plastic if used), clean it again to be safe, and lay the holster up to dry for at least two additional days.

Rubbing alcohol can be substituted for water in the above process. Slightly more costly, it is less likely to cause rusting if you were careless about oiling your gun. (No Junior, you pour the alcohol in the holster—don't try to put the holster in the bottle. Besides, I said rubbing alcohol.)

**35**

These pictures show proper positioning of gun: squarely on hip with butt straight "fore and aft" and gun perpendicular to ground with no lean or twist.

Picture on left shows front view of proper holster position. Picture on right is all wrong. Too much bend of metal insert causing butt to protrude. Will hang on draw and interferes with arm movement in walking.

A wide, heavy gun belt can be made to conform more quickly to your body by similar treatment. After soaking thoroughly, wear it tightly cinched, without gun, until it dries.

After blocking your holster as described above, you are ready to adjust it for proper hang. Buckle on the rig and stand at a position approximating "attention" in front of a large mirror. Move the position of the holster on the belt until it is in a location which feels right to you but is, within close bounds, squarely on the right hip.

Now look at your gun in the mirror. Its axis should form a straight line perpendicular to the floor. This can be corrected, if necessary, by bending the shank slightly. At this point it is well to remember that the steel shank is for the following purposes: to hold the holster stiff and lessen chance of gun hanging on the draw; to conform to the hip for comfort; and to allow adjustment of the gun position. Don't overdo the bending. The gun should form a straight line, not lean away from the body. If the shank is bent enough to follow the curve of the hip it should give ample clearance between gun butt and holster.

The other dimension to be checked is the direction in which the butt is pointing. This should be straight "fore and aft," slanting neither in nor out. This effect is easily attained by twisting the shank until the desired position results.

After these adjustments you will find that the gun, although snugly held, can be easily lifted straight out with two fingers with no binding effect and that the gun butt does not interfere with the normal swing of the arm in walking.

One last comment on the "water treatment." In time, the leather, regardless of the quality, will soften from usage. This can be remedied temporarily by soaking and allowing to dry *without* the gun. Some shrinkage occurs and the leather will be hardened in this process. Naturally, it will not hold its hardness as it did when new.

I have seen holster wells treated with a neats foot oil and graphite solution, and also with dry graphite. While this will no doubt result in a slick inside surface, it also results in a slick black coat on gun and hands where its value is even more questionable. Actually, I believe that this "improvement" would be more imaginary than real.

Our western writers love to describe the "well oiled holster" of the hero. This treatment may well be left to the pages of fiction. Oil will not only soften leather, but it will cause it to stretch just as water does. An oiled surface is also slightly "tacky" and some hanging of the gun will probably result. Wax shoe

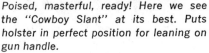

*Poised, masterful, ready! Here we see the "Cowboy Slant" at its best. Puts holster in perfect position for leaning on gun handle.*

*Result: A handfull of everything!*

polish may be applied, both for the appearance and the preservation of your leather.

Next to the application of oil as a spoiler of good leather comes the practice of "leaning" on the gun. This is an attitude, assumed mostly by younger officers, in which the entire weight of the upper body is supported by the right hand or forearm pushing down on the holstered gun. Actually, since the holster is attached to the belt, which in turn is strapped around the waist, this apparent support of the torso is more fancied than real, which can be readily proved by attempting to raise both legs. You will find that they are still supporting all of your weight, and that the only effect of the "gun leaning" is to make a bad impression on the public and stretch your holster out of shape.

With proper care a good gun rig should last for many years of hard service. Buying leather which is "just as good" with price as the criterion is poor economy. Getting the best will save you money, and maybe your life.

# Grips

THE COMPETITIVE target shooter knows well that properly designed and fitted grips will add points to his score. He lavishes time, thought and money on the selection and manufacture of his gun "handles," sometimes going to the extreme of building up monstrosities with plastic wood and electricians tape, either to be used "as is" or copied by a custom stock maker. That he would be better served by using time tested standard patterns, expertly custom fitted to his hand dimensions and formation, is beside the point. The fact that he *believes* that he has solved his grip problem is of undoubted value to his well being and might even result in improved shooting.

There is a lesson to be learned from this. A target pistol is fired by placing the weapon firmly within the shooting hand, grasping it in the approved manner, and, having first given due consideration to the niceties of foot position, breath control, and the eye or eyes to be used in aiming, carefully aligning the sights and even more carefully squeezing off a single action trigger with a two to three pound pull. All this to fire a .22 rimfire or larger caliber with reduced loads at a clearly defined bull's-eye. If custom grips are beneficial under the above conditions, consider their value to the combat shooter. Instead of the attention to detail and fine deliberation of the target shooter, he must move his hand at great speed to the gun butt—regardless of the awkward hand and body positions in which he might have been caught when the signal to go into action was received. Grasping the grip at whatever point his hand chances to contact it he completes his draw, points the weapon at the target and triggers a 15 pound or greater double action pull to fire his shot, aiming by the feel of the gun in his hand only. All these actions must be completed so rapidly as to leave little opportunity to make adjustments of grip.

Obviously, properly designed grips which fit the individual hand perfectly are much more important in firing heavy recoil weapons by feel than in the shooting of light recoil weapons under the conditions of target competition. Yet, although much thought and experimenting has gone into the making of excellent grips for target work, most of the grips offered for "combat" appear to have had little or no serious thought given to the problems involved. They

**39**

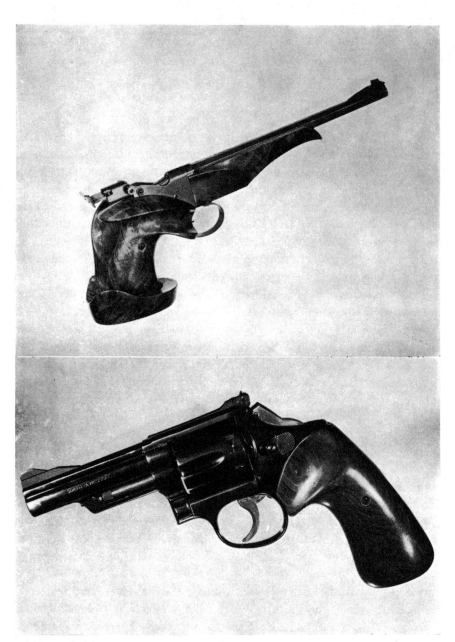

Extreme contrast in specialization. Both grips pictured are manufactured by Herretts Stocks and both are excellent designs, each to do a specific job. Above is International Slow Fire singleshot pistol by Hammerli with form fitted grips. Below is S&W Magnum with Jordan Trooper combat grips.

follow traditional designs and apparently the "designers" are more concerned with how these grips look than with whether they absorb or distribute recoil comfortably and assist in instinctive gun pointing.

To spare the guilty custom stock makers and pick on the large gun companies who are in a position to better withstand criticism, the "target" model stocks put out by S&W and Colt are typical of the design errors most commonly made. Unfortunately, most "custom combat" stocks are patterned after these commercial models; any improvements being mainly a matter of choice woods, better finish and fancy checkering.

The main design features of these grips are few and obvious: first, more wood than in standard grips; second, a built-in "filler" between grip frame and trigger guard allowing the weight of the gun to rest on the second instead of the trigger finger; third, a pronounced bulge at the top of the grip strap intended to keep the recoil of the weapon from forcing it to slip down through the hand; and fourth, a general taper from top to bottom ending in a pronounced flair at the bottom of the grips seemingly designed to *help* the recoil to force the gun to slip down through the hand. If there is any other purpose, it is not apparent. One last feature, probably added with the thought that it would afford a firm grip and dress up the whole affair, is the checkering.

Taking these items one by one and analyzing them is not encouraging. Although there is more wood than is found in the skimpy standard grips, little thought appears to have been given to whether the contour of this wood fitted *anybody's* hand. In the interest of flexibility both sides of the grips are the same, thereby fitting neither a right handed or left handed person, although making it possible for either to hold the weapon without too much danger of dropping it.

The filler is a good idea; however, it is generally constructed with a rounded surface, giving a minimum bearing on the second finger. This fairly well destroys the effectiveness of this feature, bruising the finger on the rounded ridge and on the trigger guard if heavy recoil loads are fired. The support offered is negligible.

In the matter of the bulge at the top of the grip strap, this is built into the metal in both the S&W and the Colt. Grips produced by these companies follow the line of the metal, allowing the bulge to protrude. In most custom grips where the backstrap is covered, this bulge is reproduced and even accentuated in wood. It is true that the barrel of a handgun flips up in recoil, causing a down thrust at the rear and tending to force the grips down through the hand; and it is true that an extension directly above the web between the

Contrast shown from two angles. Factory grips on left and right, combat style custom grips in center. Note the wide bearing surface of filler on the custom grips as compared to the narrow, rounded surface of the commercial "target" grips.

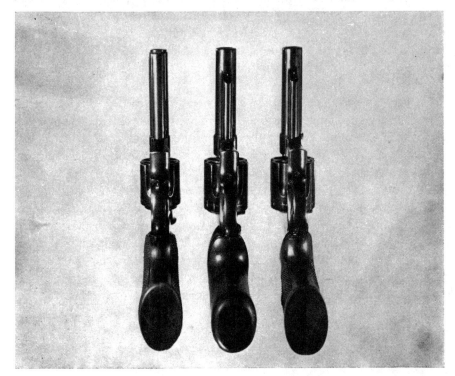

thumb and forefinger acts as a brake and tends to keep the gun from moving down. Unfortunately, it is also true that this is accomplished by directing most of the recoil to the weakest part of the hand and slamming an unyielding metal or wood projection down against the tenderest and weakest part of the hand.

Smith & Wesson target grips (top) and Colt target grips (bottom) showing bulge built into metal at top of grip strap and flared bottom of grips as contrasted to custom grips designed for double action shooting with heavy recoil weapons.

The graceful flare at the bottom of the grips has already been commented on. It appears to have been added only for looks and to counteract all the other features intended to prevent the gun from shifting in the hand, since it practically forces a downward movement from recoil.

Many years ago, dissatisfied with the grips available, I took my dissatisfaction and my thoughts on the subject to an old friend, Walter Roper. Mr. Roper was, to the best of my knowledge, the first man to make a thorough study of the subject of handgun grips. Of an inquiring mind, he was willing to

**43**

investigate any idea which appeared to have merit. Once started on a project he attacked it with patience and ingenuity, never stopping until he had tested every avenue he could conceive. Books he authored are still considered texts on the subject of handguns and their accessories. Walter made a pair of grips to my specifications, subsequently making a number of modifications to this original model until both he and I were satisfied that the desired features were built in. These features were basically as follows: a wide, contoured filler which allowed the weight of the gun to rest comfortably on the second finger and further took over the job of preventing a downward movement of the gun in the hand; a rounded contour instead of the flared butt mentioned above; and the backline of the grip forming a nearly perfect arc, dropping away toward the top and covering the bulge of the frame. These grips allowed the gun to be controlled and pointed accurately, even when a too hastily taken grip left the hand too high or too low and it moved the recoil into the palm of the hand where it belongs and can be best absorbed, instead of in the web of the hand, which is the weakest and tenderest point. These grips were made by Roper until his death, then by the late Lew Sanderson, and are now custom made by Herretts' stocks as their Jordan Trooper Model.

A feature of these stocks not previously mentioned is that they are customarily made without checkering. The uncheckered model, in my opinion, is more comfortable in firing weapons such as the .357 and .44 Magnums; and in drawing, it's smooth surface permits a last instant grip adjustment by trained fingers, which would be more difficult if the grips were rough with checkering.

Although again it might appear that the above constitutes a commercial, such is not my intention. When I first took my ideas to Mr. Roper and had them translated into wood, it was done for my own benefit and with no thought that others might be interested. It would be difficult to put these ideas on paper without describing the stocks which resulted from them. Their being manufactured commercially followed a demand for these stocks by others, instead of the usual promotion where the product is offered and a demand built through advertising. Since they were not designed commercially it is sometimes not possible for a person with a very small hand to be satisfactorily fitted with these grips for the .44 and .45 frame guns. This is regrettable, but no attempt has been, or will be, made to alter the design where desirable features would be sacrificed to increase sales.

# Fast Draw

THIS CHAPTER, while written expressly for the modern enforcement officer, may be of more than passing interest to the civilian. Fast gun handling can be a fascinating game as well as the grim difference between living and going down which it so often means to the lawman. Precision shooting has its own particular rewards, but no shooter, Master rating notwithstanding, should consider himself such on the sole basis of the deliberate single action shooting of present day match competition. Until he can draw and get his hit in times shading one half second, he should not presume that he has mastered the handgun. Nor should he assume that he is deriving all the pleasure inherent in the game of pistol shooting. There is much that he is missing.

But to return to the enforcement officer. Here the "game" element is strictly secondary. It seems beyond understanding that any peace officer could be blind to the necessity of attaining the maximum efficiency possible to him with the one tool of his trade. True, the day when the town Marshal had to shoot it out with every reputation hunting gunslinger who entered his "kingdom" is largely a thing of the past. But, make no mistake about it, that handgun jutting out so jauntily from his hip is not there as an ornament designed to give him a swashbuckling air. If he has to use it he will be playing for keeps—and on his skill will depend the lives of himself and others. There are no excuses for lack of dexterity. With only one tool to master, failure to develop efficiency with that tool to the fullest can be attributed only to lack of sincerity, laziness or stupidity. Those are hard words, but by any logic, justified.

There has been a great deal of foolishness written about fast gun work. Tales of the old time gunmen, in particular, have been exaggerated to the point of being completely ridiculous to a logical person. Nor has the modern fast draw been slighted in this respect. For some unexplained reason, it is a subject that tends to make unmitigated liars out of normally honest men. I have heard usually veracious persons, in my presence, unashamedly announce to all listeners that they had witnessed my dropping a coin, drawing, and hitting it TWICE before it hit the ground. In a case of this kind there is little that the subject can do except assume a modest expression and keep his mouth shut. If, after your well meaning booster has stated that he SAW this phenomenon

(1)

(5)

(3)

(4)

(7)

Fast draw timer. Target is cut out "K" zone of Colt Silhouette mounted on plywood backing and must be hit to stop timer. Variable time switch in control box actuates clock and lights "eyes" as signal to draw. An invaluable training aid as it teaches individual his own "plateau"; i.e., speed at which he can get a sure hit without slowing unnecessarily. Author has been timed on above equipment and on Ross "Robot Dueller" at witnessed 27/100 of second. (Reflex time and hit. Using wax bullets at ten feet.) Hit time in photograph approximately .320.

(1)                                      (2)

(5)                                      (6)

This series runs straight across to opposite page and back. Note arcing motion of hand and that all motion is of hand and arm only. Body naturally erect with no

(3)                                      (4)

(7)                                      (8)

stoop or squat. None of pictures in this book illustrating draw are "posed" they are all from sequences of draws at full speed.

with his own eyes, you should point out the physical impossibility of such a stunt (when your bullet hits the coin, it's gone!) you have gained nothing but an enemy who will hate you to his dying day, and probably swear from that time on that you are a phony who couldn't hit the proverbial bull with any kind of fiddle. Hitting a coin once is pretty fast and pretty accurate shooting, but it's just not good enough in describing a fast draw. For years, writers have described a draw of such flashing speed that the hand disappeared, or at best, was a blur too fast for the eye to follow. This belongs properly in the realm of legerdemain. The only way the human hand can move so as not to be seen is through misdirection of the attention of the viewer. Even if you swing your hand in an arc before your eyes, without giving it any of the tasks required of it in drawing and firing a gun, your eye can follow it all the way.

This confused reporting on the part of spectators, coupled with over-stimulated imaginations and the leavening effect of the passage of time, has caused a veil of mystery to be drawn around the fast draw, thus concealing its factual identity. The really fast men have been made to appear superhuman and their feats impossible of emulation by the average person. Discouraged by this false standard, very few make more than a half-hearted and shortlived attempt to learn to draw. Instead of starting with fundamentals and gradually conditioning their reflexes to the muscle-memory patterns which must be developed before speed can be attained, the usual practice is to immediately try to make the fastest draw possible. This invariably results in a bruised hand and a chastened spirit, and, mentally comparing his blundering attempts to the mythical perfection of the old gun fighters, one more would-be fast draw artist resigns himself to the impossibility of his attaining such a goal.

The point I am trying to make is this: Any man with normal reflexes and coordination can master fast draw double action shooting. But first he must make a drastic downgrading of his pre-conceived notions of what is humanly possible of accomplishment, lest he lose heart before he starts. There are only two factors upon which the speed of a draw is dependent: the physical make-up of the individual and the economy of motion which can be achieved. We will go into the mechanics, that is, the economy of motion required, later, but first let us take up the item of physical make-up.

It would be as ridiculous to claim that any person can become fast enough to make draws in the one fifth to two fifth second bracket of the top men as it would be to state categorically that any man can learn to run the mile in four minutes. Similar factors govern both tests. All of us do not possess the lightning reflexes and muscular coordination of the champions. But do not forget, that, just as these four-minute milers finish only a short distance ahead of the "also-ran's" in comparison to the total distance covered, so also do the fastest men on the draw have only a slight edge on the average trained man in this field. In fact, in fast draw work, the times involved are so infinitesimal that it is often impossible to differentiate visually between a record draw and one that took nearly twice as long. And the difference is so slight that the average man can develop his ability to the point where the only factor in determining the winner of a gun fight between himself and the fastest gunman who ever lived (psychology not being taken into consideration) would probably be simply who started for his gun first. Don't believe it? Then, figure it out for yourself. The mechanical limit for ANY human to draw and hit a target representing the vital area of a man's body, under realistic conditions, is from two to four tenth seconds. I make this statement with confidence, despite recently reported times less than two tenths in which blanks were fired actuating a timer by concussion. Such records I consider without meaning since no accuracy was involved. The history of gun fighting fails to record a single fatality resulting from a quick noise. Below two tenths the vanishing point of NO elapsed time is practically reached. It is doubtful that any of the old timers ever attained a speed of three tenths second. That figure and below is possible only to modern guns and holsters and then only if the signal to draw originates with the man making the draw, that is, the timing begins when his hand starts to move. If time is started with an external signal it will take that same man from about three tenths to one full second or over to draw, depending on the degree of surprise involved, with the average time running six tenths or above. Now, suppose you can draw and fire in six tenths of a second—comparatively slow time and well within your capabilities—and he STARTED to draw when he saw your hand move?

If by now your interest and ambition is aroused, let's go into details on how you are going to reach that six tenths second speed.

It is assumed that you are well grounded in the fundamentals of slow fire, single action revolver shooting. If you are not, fast draw double action shooting is still in the future for you. It is in the nature of post-graduate work for well grounded shooters. So—if you can't shoot consistent tens on a regulation target—file this away for future reference until you have mastered those fundamentals. You can't expect to run until you have learned to walk.

The mechanics involved in getting a handgun into action in the fastest possible time are simply that the fewest and shortest movements be used, and

(1)

(2)

(5)

(6)

52

(3)

(4)

(7)

Draw sequence from different angle. Note that the arcing motion is apparent. Also that shoulder drops slightly back so that weapon may be leveled and fired without strain in shortest possible motion. In all illustrations draw started from hand high position to accentuate illustration of arc.

(1)  (2)

(5)  (6)

Draw from under coat without side sway. It may be noted that coat does not clear hand as well as if started moving by swaying hips as illustrated on pages 58 and 59.

(3)                                                        (4)

that the hand, once in motion, continue that motion without pause until the weapon is lined on the target and the shot is fired. In order that this efficiency be attained, four cardinal points are vital to success:

1. Relax.
2. Let shoulder drop back in drawing.
3. Keep body motionless and draw with arm movement only.
4. Use circular, or arcing, motion of hand.

1. In instructing you to relax, lack of muscular tension is implied. Certainly there will be no attempt to tell you how to be relaxed in the face of a gun fight, or even an exhibition of your skill before an audience. That would be expecting too much of any intelligent nervous system. Here we are dealing only with trying to attain the greatest possible speed, commensurate with accuracy, that can be reached under ideal conditions—at such short ranges that a hit can be registered on a large target while the gun is in motion. As a matter of fact, nervous tension seems to act as a spur to the speed of your reflexes provided muscular tension can be avoided. At least, there should be no conscious stiffening of the arm, hand and shoulder muscles, but rather all possible looseness of these parts should be attempted.

2. The right shoulder should be allowed to drop slightly back in the act of drawing as opposed to the exaggerated forward thrust advocated by some

*"Gunman's crouch"* contrasted with straight up stance. While presenting somewhat smaller target, this advantage is more than offset by loss of time. Quickness of erect position could prevent your presenting any kind of target.

methods of teaching. This is a point which you can easily prove for yourself. If you will slowly draw a gun, using the exaggerated forward thrust of the shoulder, you will find that the weapon cannot be leveled until it is well in front of the body. Dropping the shoulder back instead, allows the gun to be pointed at the target just as it clears the holster, an economy of motion which reduces slightly the overall time. And remember that here we are dealing in split seconds and that everything saved counts. If you fire a burst, you will find that the hand will naturally extend further with each successive shot, giving a slight increase of accuracy for any new targets to come under fire, but without any loss of speed for that vital first shot. In this connection, the theory has been advanced by this "shoulder thrust" school that the first shot should be fired as soon as the gun clears the holster, whether lined up on the target or not. (This is not the matter of deliberately holding low where the target is not clear due to poor light conditions.) The idea of this being that even if those first shots only plow up the dirt between yourself and your opponent they will disconcert him and cause him to miss. In my opinion this theory defeats the whole idea of fast draw marksmanship, which, when reduced to its essentials, is simply to place your shot in a vital spot before you are hit by your opponent. Surely nothing could be more disconcerting to the accuracy of an adversary than a .357 Magnum slug applied judiciously in the region of his belt buckle! It will beat kicking dirt in his face every time! No man can afford to spot an opponent the two or three, or even one wasted shots advocated by the exponents of this hair brained theory. There is an old adage which should be held in mind at all times as you work on the fast draw: "Speed's fine but accuracy's final." I do not know who first made that statement, but he was a very *sabe hombre*. There is too much fancy gun juggling being masqueraded as fast gun work. If you cannot hit your target on the first shot you had best give up the quest for speed until you can. Always remember, it is the first shot on target that counts. Not necessarily the first shot fired. In practice, your speed should never be allowed to get ahead of your accuracy.

3. The body should remain motionless and the draw made with the arm only. The rigid claw-like fingers and the gunman's crouch so often seen on movie and TV screens and described by Western writers, while both menacing and impressive, are no part of an efficient fast draw technique. In regard to this crouch another fatuous theory has been advanced. It makes a smaller target of you and if you are hit you will not be knocked backward, but instead will fall forward, thereby being enabled to continue firing enroute! As to the smaller target, that has been a point of argument from time immemorial.

(1)         (2)

(5)         (6)

*Series illustrating the draw from under coat using sway of hips to start coat away from body. Series runs across to facing page.*

(3)

(4)

(7)

(8)

Duelists of the eighteenth and nineteenth centuries held opposing views on this. One school advocated standing sidewise to an antagonist to lessen the target area. The opponents of this idea pointed out that this would make it probable that a hit would pierce both lungs instead of one as would be the case if the duelist faced his adversary squarely. The question is unresolved to this day. As to the matter of falling forward when hit; Well, now! It is hard to imagine that defeatist attitude as part of the credo of John Wesley Hardin or Wyatt Earp! There is no point in developing superior skill with a firearm if the issue is to be settled by the superior ability to absorb shock on the part of the winner rather than by the use of that superior skill. There are three good reasons for the upright stance: There is no strained, unnatural position of the body to hamper smooth movement of the arm; your intentions are not disclosed by "telegraphing your punch" as they would be by assuming a menacing crouch; and, after training your hand to a specific task of going instinctively to the same place, the gun will be at that place rather than having to be pursued and caught in movement.

4. The fourth point is probably the most important. The hand must not pause from the moment it starts moving until the instant the gun is fired. The only means by which this can be accomplished is that the hand move in a circular motion, "scooping" up the revolver enroute. The importance of eliminating this stopping of the gun hand cannot be overemphasized. Aside from the fact that a fraction of time is lost while the hand is actually stopped, it is an indisputable fact that any movement of the hand is slowest during its earliest stages, momentum being gained as the motion continues. Unless a circular motion is used, the draw becomes two motions, each with its period of overcoming the inertia of any motionless object: And since in the second stage there are two objects, the hand and a heavy gun, to start moving again, the speed of the entire operation is measurably delayed. This is the factor which constitutes the difference between the top gun hand and the efficient but slower second rater. The speed with which the hand can be made to move and reflexes respond represents in whole that difference, since each can attain the same proficiency in the actual mechanics of the draw.

With one exception, the technique of drawing from under a coat, as plain clothes officers must, is the same in all essentials as the draw of an unconcealed gun. Here a sway of the hips or short step to the left starts the coat moving away from the right hip and the little finger edge of the hand striking against the coat continues that movement until the coat is brushed aside, the hand continuing in a circular motion as in a normal draw. Naturally, the hand must be in front of the forward edge of the coat at the start of the draw. In this situation the advantage gained by starting the coat away from the hip overbalances the disadvantage of moving the hip and thereby having to "chase the gun." A good stunt is to carry a few cartridges in the right coat pocket. When the hips are swayed the weight of these cartridges will make the movement of the coat more sluggish and hold it out away from the body a little longer, facilitating completion of the draw. In all other respects the mechanics described herein apply.

With the foregoing points in mind you are now ready to start dry practice. That, of course, is the secret of developing a fast draw. Through hard practice alone will you be able to perfect your technique in slow motion, striving always for smoothness. Regardless of the starting position of your hand, make its movement continuous. With thumbs hooked in belt, your hand describes a circle. From hanging by your side it goes forward or back and up in an arc, depending on starting position. From a "hands up" position, down and around in a circle. Always one movement. This practice can be performed before a mirror with profit for there you can see any deviation from the desired pattern of minimum movement of the hand in its circular path. There too you can see that the gun is raised only barely enough to clear the holster before it is snapped into alignment with the target and whether it is pointed properly at the completion of the draw. On each draw the trigger should be pulled starting with the time your hand touches the gun and continuing smoothly as the draw progresses to the point that the hammer will fall at the exact instant the muzzle first lines up with the target. Only after your reflexes are so disciplined that you instinctively draw and point the gun with one smooth, fluid motion should you attempt to increase your speed. And then let the increase be gradual. Never sacrifice smoothness for forced speed. It is a snare and a delusion. You think you are drawing faster but the smooth draw with no waste motion is always best. And you will find that in time you will have that speed without straining. Your hand will unerringly cuddle the grip, your trigger finger will find the trigger and start its pull, and the gun will fire at the very instant it is on the target.

Do not allow yourself to become impatient with the dry-fire routine. An attempt to try your wings too soon with a loaded gun can well lead to disaster. It is not difficult to shoot oneself in the leg or some other more intimate part of the anatomy. It has been done. You start your draw, your finger engages the trigger and starts pulling, the gun catches and stops momentarily and the trigger finger keeps going. This is known as being slow on the draw and fast on

High speed photography catches finger action at moment of hands contact with gun. Note small and ring fingers beginning to curl around grip in number one—completing this movement in two—and in three how closing of middle finger has pulled trigger finger into guard and in contact with trigger.

the trigger, and, unless you wish to develop the three-toed limp of the typical Hollywood "gunslinger," should be avoided! Aside from the danger, use of actual loads will impede your progress. Instinctively you will pause after the gun has cleared the holster and then pull instead of carrying through the "draw and fire in one motion" routine you have been practicing. Before going to normal loads and for most of your practice, wax bullets, impelled by the primer only, should be used. A prudent man will not rely upon hip shooting at distances greater than seven yards, the practical limit of fast gunmanship. Beyond this distance the pistol should be brought up toward eye level as the range increases until at the longer ranges it is fired by looking down the barrel or actually using the sights. These squib loads are amazingly accurate up to twenty or twenty-five feet, they practically eliminate the element of danger, and they build up confidence so that you will let the shot go without hesitation. If you are unable to make or otherwise procure any of these wax loads the next best practice is to always fire two fast shots; the first an empty cylinder and the second a live round. Thus, if an accident should happen the hammer will fall on an unloaded cylinder. If all goes well, the second shot will give you the information desired as to the accuracy of your gun pointing.

Any good revolver is satisfactory for fast draw work, provided the double action is smooth. Barrel length should be between three and five inches, with four inches probably the ideal length. A heavy barrel is preferable to one of

**62**

lighter weight since for point shooting it gives a "feel" to the weapon which is not present when the weight is all in the hand. Some type of ramp with a forward slanting, smooth sight should be used to avoid gouging the holster and dragging. The only other items of equipment which will add to speed and accuracy are custom grips, designed for double action shooting with heavy recoil guns and well designed, high quality leather. These items are discussed in detail in other chapters of this book.

In practicing the fast draw, the point which should always be carried uppermost in mind is the fact that it is dangerous. The danger to yourself has already been mentioned. It is even more dangerous to others. There is something about the subject, probably the fact that each of us retain a little of the "Cowboy and Indians" spirit of boyhood, which brings out overenthusiasm. It hardly seems necessary to point out the thoroughness with which the gun should be unloaded before dry practice. Take out the loads, count them and put them in your pocket. Then open the gun again for another look. Most men will follow this routine religiously. It is after practice and the reloading of the gun that the period of greatest danger begins. Then is when that enthusiasm gets the best of you. You forget that the gun is reloaded and make one more practice draw; or there is a bull session about drawing and you want to illustrate a point or demonstrate the flashing speed you have developed. The resulting loud noise is most disconcerting in a closed room, even if the consequences are not more serious. One habit, if unfailingly adhered to, will prevent such an accident from ever happening. As soon as you have reloaded and returned the gun to the holster, fasten the safety strap as part of that operation and KEEP IT SNAPPED until you have left the scene and your mind is thoroughly engrossed with some other subject. Then if you try to make another draw you will be reminded forcibly that you have reloaded and that practice is over for the time being. The gun cannot be drawn and you will be saved either remorse or embarrassment.

Fast draw and point shooting are important skills of the enforcement officer. Statistics show that affrays between officers and criminals usually occur under conditions of surprise, short range, and poor light. Conditions which make deliberate, aimed fire not only inadvisable but impossible. That so many officers are inclined to view their deficiencies in these skills with complacency is alarming. This attitude may have been influenced by the game of Quick Draw which has attained considerable popularity in recent years. Here, the speed with which a gun can be drawn and fired is, in itself, an end, rather than a means to an end. That this pastime should be so lightly regarded by an officer as to cause him to dismiss all fast draw practice as a game beneath the dignity of a grown man is an indication that the officer is not thinking clearly on the subject. A fast draw is only the first part, albeit a very important part, of the process of getting a quick hit on an opponent. Its mastery is just as important today as it was in the 1870's. This is being proved every day; positively by survival and negatively by the death of an officer. Police records all over the country verify this statement. On the negative side, a typical example was reported in today's newspaper. Two officers answered the routine call "go to apartment house, corner of Blank and Central, man beating his wife." Climbing the stairs to the indicated apartment they looked up into the barrel of a .22 pistol in the hand of a psycho on the landing above. Caught by surprise and expecting no violence, both were shot down by an unbalanced, inept amateur. Although we will never know, it appears probable that, had they been trained "fast draw artists," at least one of these officers should have been able to draw and shoot before he was shot down. Another case, on the positive side, happened within my own service so recently that the officer involved is still convalescing. Since it not only points up the value of being able to draw and shoot fast and accurately, but also graphically demonstrates another commodity, determination, extolled elsewhere in this work as a requisite of survival, I feel that the details are sufficiently illustrative and interesting to bear repeating.

Senior Patrol Inspector Darwin Earle is Inspector in Charge of the Mercedes, Texas, station of the U. S. Border Patrol. On the night of July 24, 1964, he was seriously wounded under the following circumstances: After observing the disposition of his evening shift teams on line watch near Mercedes, Earle, who was working alone on back up patrol, had stopped near the intersection of a levee and a trail much used by smugglers and wetbacks. Observing two men on the levee silhouetted against the faint moonlight, Earle took up a position on the trail designed to intercept their course. Since this appeared to be a routine "wetback" apprehension with little danger involved, Inspector Earle did not draw his gun. However, he took the precaution of checking to see that the safety strap was snapped out of the way on the back of the holster. Waiting for the man in the lead to pass him, he ordered the two to halt. The first man, who was apparently carrying a gun in his hand, without warning, whirled and fired one shot from a distance of about six feet. The bullet struck Earle in the lower abdomen, going on through and hitting his right hip bone. This probably saved the Inspector's life, since the shock of the bullet hitting bone caused him to fall sideways due to the crumpling of his right leg.

As he was falling he drew and fired three shots at his assailant before he struck the ground. All three shots, either of which would have proved almost instantly fatal, took effect and the man fell into a ditch. The second man ran south in the direction from which he had come.

Inspector Earle, badly wounded, crawled back to his vehicle, losing consciousness several times enroute. Though the distance was only 105 steps it required over thirty minutes for him to reach the Scout, pull himself into the driver's seat and radio for help. His case was complicated in that the vehicle was parked in a radio "dead spot" and he was forced to start the motor and move a few yards before he could get an answer. He was then able to drive the Scout back to the roadway before again becoming unconscious.

The deceased alien, who was carrying a package of marijuana in his other hand, was identified as Cosme Cuellar-Cuellar, a notorious, vicious, criminal, who had amassed a total of 198 years in prison sentences for crimes of burglary and assault. He had been described by the Cameron County Sheriff's Office as the "Valley's Public Enemy No. 1." His operations were trade-marked by brutality as he invariably beat, shot or stabbed his robbery victims. All in all, he was a far cry from the routine arrest that Inspector Earle was expecting to make.

Taking into consideration the violent character of the criminal, it is apparent that he was coolly waiting for Earle to fall to the ground and cease moving so that he could be surer of hitting his target with follow-up shots. His mistake was that he underestimated the speed and the determination of the officer he had shot. Anyone knowing Inspector Earle could have told him that this officer did not know how to give up. As for his underestimating the speed with which retribution would overtake him, he should have known from a reputation forty years in the building that the officers of the U. S. Border Patrol are tough, fast, and accurate. Unfortunately for Cuellar, most of the *contrabandistas* who could have told him this were not talking.

It is clear that here, in a setting as modern as today, an officer would have died if he had not been fast and sure with his gun and if he had not continued to fight, even after being seriously wounded.

It has been said that the fastest draw is to have the gun in your hand when trouble seems imminent. Though plausible on the surface, such advice is patently impractical. Unless you are the owner of a highly accurate Ouija Board or crystal ball, this would necessitate your carrying a six-shooter in your hand at all times to be on the safe side. A practice the general public, and your Chief, would not be inclined to view kindly. If you KNOW that you are in for a fight, it might be an advantage. But the confidence inspired by your knowledge of what you can do with a gun if necessary is bound to be reflected in your bearing. It is a confidence that cannot be counterfeited. Either you have it or you don't. If you do, it will be sensed by an enemy, causing doubt to arise in his mind; and a feeling of personal doubt will adversely affect his actions in a situation where loss of any advantage might be fatal. It will enable you to go through many a tough spot with a poise and presence of mind which may avert the actual opening of hostilities which would surely follow either a show of force or lack of confidence on your part. The statement that having a gun in your hand in advance is always a great advantage is open to question unless it is a shotgun which understandably stifles all initiative in the opposition! Aside from being an "overt act" which would probably "open the ball" unnecessarily, the slightest distraction of attention, such as turning the eyes to check a noise or movement, is long enough for a fast man to bring his hands down and kill that fellow with the "drop" before he can fire the gun in his hand. Once again a matter of getting the jump on his reflexes.

In the final analysis, it is the unexpected situation that packs the most danger for an officer, and it is in such situations that fast draw gunmanship pays off. So get in front of that mirror and start practicing.

# Sidearms

A HANDGUN bears the same relation to a law enforcement officer that a hammer does to a carpenter. It is the tool and symbol of his trade. That this analogy is by no means perfect is quite evident. When the carpenter makes a mistake he pulls the bent nail and drives a new one. In cases requiring the use of his "tool" the officer seldom gets a second chance. His mistake is, more often than not, final.

If the analogy is not perfect, neither is the tool. Where an officer knew that he was heading into trouble, certainly the handgun would not be his choice of weapons. It is difficult to shoot well, inherently inaccurate (as compared to a rifle), and lacking in power. Probably his first choice would be a shotgun. There we have the most efficient tranquilizer ever developed. Or, if a shotgun was not available, then a rifle would get the nod over a handgun. Unfortunately, such prior knowledge is seldom available, so we come back to the original premise: The handgun is the tool of the peace officer's trade. It, and it alone, will probably be his sole companion when the chips are down. What it lacks in the other virtues are overbalanced by its portability and availability.

Indispensability conceded, let's take a look at what is available. There are three basic types of handgun, each with some claim to consideration by the officer: These are the single action revolver, the semi-auto, and the double action.

The single action, with its classic lines and colorful background has a strong appeal; however, this appeal is more nostalgic than practical. Despite tales of its ruggedness, the single action trigger mechanism is the most delicate of the three and easily put out of action or rendered unsafe. Other drawbacks are that only five rounds may be safely carried in the cylinder and reloading is a very slow process. Although, in the hands of an expert, the single action can probably be drawn and fired faster than any other weapon, this extreme speed can only be attained if accuracy is disregarded. The technique is difficult to master; and, of course, after that first shot, the speed and accuracy with which succeeding shots can be delivered cannot be compared with either the automatic or the double action. This statement is made in the full knowledge that

**67**

"fanning"—a form of suicide practiced by make believe gunfighters—is a very rapid method of burning gunpowder. The single action cannot be seriously considered by a working peace officer.

Second on our list is the automatic. (Yeah, I know. We'll call it the "automatic" anyway, just like everyone else does.) Here we have two strong

The Great Tranquilizer! Sawed off shotgun used in illustration and on frontispiece was made by Ithica for the Wells Fargo Company. From the collection of Dr. John Palmer of Brownsville, Texas.

points, both related to firepower. The automatic carries more rounds in the magazine and can be reloaded with spare clips more rapidly than any other type of handgun. As a military weapon against a massed *banzai* attack, it would be hard to beat. Its greatest disadvantages are that it is slow for the first shot, is not in most models a natural "pointer," and is limited in the power of the loads which are available. In models which can be fired double action the first shot is appreciably speeded, but the action of none of these can be compared with the smooth action of a quality double action revolver. Where the double action feature is not present, some automatic users attempt to make a more rapid first shot possible by carrying the weapon in the holster cocked, with the thumb safety on. While I am aware that there are other safety devices and that, theoretically at least, this is a safe practice, I have never seen a gun so

Above: The three basic types of handguns. Reading from top to bottom: Single action; Auto-loader; and Double action. The double action is the type best suited for service use in Law Enforcement.

*A well designed holster for the .45 Auto*

carried without a momentary feeling that the man had forgot something!

I am told that in some combat style matches the .45 auto is presently enjoying considerable popularity and success. This does not particularly surprise me, but neither does it do anything to weaken my conviction that it is not a practical defense weapon for law enforcement. I *would* be surprised to learn that a serious competitor in a match requiring a fast draw and accurate first shot was using an automatic on which the grip safety had not been deactivated. I would certainly question the judgement of an officer who knowingly carried an automatic into a combat situation without first taking care of that little matter. In a hurry, you don't always get a perfect grip—particularly on a slabsided varmint like the .45 auto. Failure to have the hand in proper position to depress the grip safety could wipe you out in a match before you got started. As to the result of such a mistake in a gun fight . . . well, no comment seems necessary.

There are other respects in which the automatic fails as a police weapon. It was designed to shoot a round nosed, full jacket bullet. Since no full jacketed handgun bullet I have ever seen was worth a tinker's dam for combat, a lead, semi-wadcutter load is indicated. I have used a number of .45 automatics, altered for semi-wadcutter target loads, for match shooting. These weapons reliably handled the bullet and powder charge, for which each had been altered and tuned, with only a very occasional jam which made me think that the calculated risk of a malfunction in a match was justified . . . a risk I would not have wanted to run if the target was going to shoot back . . . however, each of these weapons was modified by many hours of intensive work by a master gunsmith and each was quite sensitive to any change in diet. To make an automatic qualify for police use, a suitable load would have to be handloaded (the only lead wadcutter commercially available is in a light target load), and each weapon tailored to fit that load, both for accuracy and for functioning reliability. While this might be done by an intensely interested individual, it would not be feasible on a departmental basis. Only loads and weapons which can be purchased by contract or bought "over the counter" can be considered as practical or satisfactory for a police organization.

All of which leads me to the conclusion that: 1. The automatic is a fine military weapon due to its firepower and fast reloading, but it has unreliable first shot speed unless the grip safety is tied down and it would be unsafe so altered. (Particularly with a big custom extension on the thumb safety); 2. It lacks sufficient shocking power with full metal jacketed bullets but would not function with complete reliability with semi-wadcutter lead bullets; 3. It is not a good natural pointer; and 4. To be modified to make it more suitable for police work would require that it become a custom item, both as to weapon and ammunition.

This brings us to the logical choice and most widely used police weapon, the double action revolver. Here, in my opinion, is the closest to the ideal for enforcement officer use presently available. Fast for the first and succeeding shots, safe and dependable, it also points well for double action hip shooting. Used single action for deliberate, aimed shots it can be effective against man-sized targets at 200 yards and beyond. There is a wide range of loads available, including the powerful Magnums.

The double action feature can be improved by smoothing all the working parts and lightening some of the springs. The smoothing can be done by any amateur with time, sweat and crocus cloth. The springs are another problem. The mainspring should never be lightened. Positive ignition is more important than weight of pull. Some of the coil springs, such as the trigger return spring in the Smith & Wesson, can be shortened to advantage. Be sure you have extra springs available in case you clip off one turn too many. The only other alterations necessary or advisable are cutting off the hammer spur, rounding the corners of the rear sight in adjustable sight models, and cutting away about half of the width of the forward part of the trigger guard on the trigger finger side. This forward part of the guard should not be entirely removed for several reasons: The remainder of the guard can become bent, jamming the trigger; the finger can catch the tip of this cutaway guard, making a shift of finger position necessary before the trigger can be pulled; and most important, it is a danger-

Trigger guard cut away. In a cold country where bulky gloves are a necessity this mutilation might be justified.

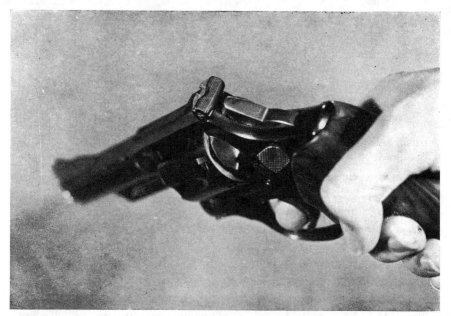

Above: Details of "de-horned" hammer and rounded rear sight are shown in this illustration. These are among the few "mutilations" which have merit. Weapon may still be easily fired by starting hammer back double action far enough to allow a good thumb hold and finish cocking single action. Alterations here shown may prevent a cut hand and can prevent hanging or tearing coat when worn with plain clothes.

Below: Trigger guard on left has been slimmed by cutting away part of the guard on trigger finger side and rounding smoothly. This allows finger to slide in smoothly and as quickly as if entire front of guard had been cut away without the danger or other disadvantages of that operation.

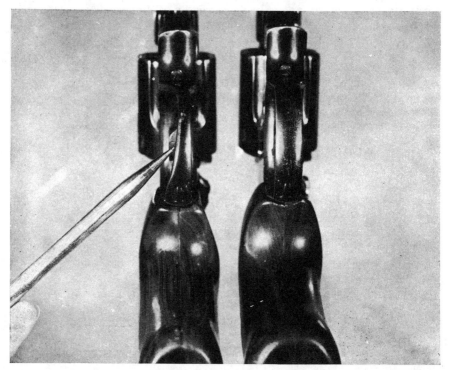

GREAT GUNS! The finest made anywhere in the world! With any of these beauties an officer is well equipped. Reading from top to bottom: Smith & Wesson Combat Magnum (.357); Smith & Wesson .44 Magnum (Made in same frame for .357 Magnum); Colt Three Fifty Seven (357 Magnum) and Colt Python (.357 Magnum.)

ous alteration. That trigger guard was not put there as an ornament. Reducing the width of this forward portion by about half and rounding it smoothly serves the same purpose as would its removal, without the disadvantages of that operation. Cutting off the hammer spur and rounding the corners of the rear sight prevent damage to the hand in drawing, and remove projections which might possibly become caught on clothing. These "mutilations" should be judiciously considered before being undertaken, with a thought to the resale effect of these operations on a gun you might wish later to dispose of. Some thought should also be given to the temperament of your chief before attempting any such alteration on an issue weapon.

For many years officers, as a whole, favored five and six inch barrel lengths. There are advantages inherent in these longer barrels. They deliver appreciably higher velocities with the same loads and point better than the short barrels due to the "feel" of those extra inches out where they count; and, of course, for aimed shots the longer sight radius means more accurate alignment. There is no appreciable difference in speed of draw. Studies of photographs taken of high speed draws show that, although every effort is made to barely clear the holster, the very force used invariably causes several inches of excess barrel clearance.

These advantages of the longer barrel, although desirable, yielded to the practical requirement of comfort in carrying with the change in law enforcement operating procedures. When the officer patrolled on foot or on horseback, the length of his barrel was no bother. Now however, with nearly all patrolling done by car or jeep, the longer barrel guns are pushed up by the seat and cause discomfort to the officer. The popularity of competitions over combat courses for police, such as the Indiana University Shoot, has caused comment by writers who noted that the high scorers almost invariably use six inch barreled guns; that the man with a four inch barrel was outgunned. There has even been some prophecy that enforcement agencies would go back to the longer barrels. I feel that these prophecies are premature. The seers are overlooking the fact that the competitors they have been admiring are playing a game in which hits in the ten and "X" rings are required to win. An officer can win in a gun fight with hits somewhat more widely dispersed than will result from the difference in accuracy of shooting long or short barrels. One eight-hour shift with the gun butt poking into the floating ribs should be sufficient to convince the most biased that the four inch barrel is here to stay.

In this country we are fortunate that we have available to us the finest double action weapons made in the world: The .357 Combat Magnum; the heavy frame .357 Magnum and the .44 Magnum, as manufactured by Smith & Wesson; the Colt Python, and Three Fifty Seven models. Better guns cannot be bought at any price, anywhere. You can't go wrong with one of these hanging by your side.

# Calibers and Loads

ALTHOUGH THE .357 Magnum is a close approach, in my opinion the ideal caliber for enforcement work is not presently available in a suitable loading. This "ideal" when presented will be the .41 caliber loaded to between 1200 and 1300 F/S with a 200 grain semi-wadcutter bullet.

The present "standard" for police agencies is the .38 Special. This is a highly developed cartridge of superb accuracy which is at its best on a target range in wadcutter loadings. As a police load it leaves much to be desired. Charitably, it can be said that it fulfills the minimum requirements. Any less powerful cartridge should not be considered except for specialized usage. Even in souped-up hand loads the best the .38 Special can boast is that it "approaches" the .357 Magnum.

The best cartridges for the automatics are the .45 Colt automatic and the 9 mm loads. Hand-loaded with semi-wadcutter lead bullets they are adequate from the standpoint of shock but do not function reliably. In factory loadings with the full metal jacket bullets available, they function reliably but are relatively ineffective.

In the Big Bertha class are the hand-loaded .45 Colt and .44 Special Cartridge and the .44 Magnum. These loads leave nothing to be desired from the standpoint of effectiveness. A solid hit with either will suspend hostilities indefinitely. Unfortunately, they are almost equally severe on the shooter's end. The heavy recoil and loud report are conducive to flinching in all but the most hardened shooter, and particularly with the .44 Magnum, recoil is so great that recovery is difficult and a second shot, if necessary, cannot be fired quickly. Although it is not likely that a second shot *would* be necessary to dispose of a person clobbered with this cannon, the possibility that he might have a friend should not be overlooked. These loads are unnecessarily powerful.

The .357 Magnum is presently the best cartridge available. With the 160 grain bullet in 4-inch barrels it delivers slightly over 1200 F/S in the factory loading and an authoritative 500 plus foot pounds of energy. While a little more shock power would be desirable, no other available cartridge is so near the ideal for police use. As an added advantage .38 Special loads can be fired

Comparative recoil of .38 Special (upper left), .357 Magnum (lower left) and .44 Magnum (upper right). It will be noted that recoil of .38 Special is hardly apparent. This comment also applies to the shock delivered by this load. By comparison, observe that the recoil of the .44 Magnum has actually moved entire body of shooter. The facial expression was involuntary, due to shock of recoil, but pretty well expresses feeling of the shooter.

These pictures illustrate that recoil moves a weapon much less when fired from hip than from target shooting position.

*S & W Chief Special Airweight, .38 Spl. caliber. This is a fine hideout gun due to its fire power, small size and negligible weight. Would be ideal in .22 RFM caliber.*

in the .357, thus cutting the expense of practice substantially. As a matter of fact, it is probable that the average owner of a .357 Magnum will shoot hundreds of .38 Special rounds through his gun for every Magnum round fired. This leads to the conclusion that the lighter ".41 frame" revolvers should be given preference over the heavy frame models. The S&W Combat Magnum, for instance, is lighter and consequently more comfortable to carry than the heavy Magnum. It has a faster, smoother action due to the difference in cylinder weight. In effect, you have in one a heavy .357 Magnum which will fire .38 Special loads, and in the other a light .38 Special which will fire the Magnum load. While this is true of the .357 in which the recoil is mild enough to be handled comfortably by the lighter weapon, it is most emphatically not true of the bigger calibers. Here plenty of recoil absorbing weight is a necessity to comfort and accuracy.

The one light loading that I would like to see would be the airweight model Cobras and Chief Specials chambered for the new .22 RF Magnum load. This is a wicked little cartridge and would add little to the weight of the light models (five .38 Special cartridges weigh about as much as the Chief airweight), and would make a wonderful addition to the "hide-out" field, particularly for officers working in hot countries where usually a coat is not worn during the hot summer months.

*Elmer Keith figures that anybody who doesn't enjoy shooting a mild recoil load like the .44 Magnum is a plumb sissy. Here he lets one go that even he doesn't consider on the weak side: .45–70 in Remington factory loading consisting of 405 grain slug on top of a large Texas jigger of black powder.*

These small, light guns have a definite value in plain clothes work. Every officer who is either assigned that duty or is considered to be in constant duty status and expected to carry a gun at all times would be well advised to own one. They are about the same size but lighter than the Derringers which are coming back into some popularity; safer, and have more firepower. When on duty and wearing a coat I prefer to carry my regular service .357 Magnum. Off duty, or when the weather is hot, there is great temptation to conclude that there won't be any trouble anyway, and go unarmed rather than to either wear a coat or look conspicuous wearing a big gun without the coat to conceal it. That's the time when the little airweight model, slipped into a trouser pocket, is

Charlie Askins, one time Border Patrolman and National Pistol Champ, pleads guilty to Elmer's charge . . . furnished his own caption for this picture: "Who the hell says the .44 Magnum kicks!?"

worth its weight in gold. And for such use the smallest and lightest gun available, provided it has reasonable power, is the best.

A recent letter from Doug Hellstrom, Smith and Wesson's dynamic young executive vice-president, says that they are working on the problems attendant to marrying the .22 RF Magnum to the Chief airweight—and there are lots of problems. Aluminum cylinder and barrel with steel liners are indicated to keep down weight. The big problem, however, is devising a method to keep the hot gases from eating through the aluminum frame above the junction of cylinder and barrel. If this problem can be whipped it should result in the perfect hideout gun. It will not only outreach a switch blade, but will pack plenty of close range authority into an easily carried and concealed package.

Just before sending this book to press, data has arrived on the long awaited .41 Magnum. In company with many other officers, as well as gun writers, I have urged the need of this load. It should fill the gap between the .357

**79**

# COMPARATIVE BALLISTICS

| .45 ACP | | .44 MAGNUM | | .44 SPECIAL | | .38 SPECIAL | |
|---|---|---|---|---|---|---|---|
| Bullet Diameter | .4515 in. | Bullet Diameter | .430 in. | Bullet Diameter | .431 in. | Bullet Diameter | .359 in. |
| Bullet Weight | 230 gr. | Bullet Weight | 240 gr. | Bullet Weight | 246 gr. | Bullet Weight | 158 gr. |
| Bullet Type | FMC | Bullet Type | L.G.C. | Bullet Type | L. | Bullet Type | L. |
| Barrel | 5 in. | Barrel | 6½ in. | Barrel | 6½ in. | Barrel | 6 in. |
| Muzzle Velocity | 850 f.s. | Muzzle Velocity | 1470 f.s. | Muzzle Velocity | 755 f.s. | Muzzle Velocity | 855 f.s. |
| Muzzle Energy | 369 f.p. | Muzzle Energy | 1150 f.p. | Muzzle Energy | 311 f.p. | Muzzle Energy | 256 f.p. |

| .41 MAGNUM J. | | .41 MAGNUM L. | | .357 MAGNUM | |
|---|---|---|---|---|---|
| Bullet Diameter | .410 in. | Bullet Diameter | .410 in. | Bullet Diameter | .359 in. |
| Bullet Weight | 210 gr. | Bullet Weight | 210 gr. | Bullet Weight | 158 gr. |
| Bullet Type | J.S.P. | Bullet Type | L.G.C. | Bullet Type | L. |
| Barrel | 8⅜ in. | Barrel | 8⅜ in. | Barrel | 8⅜ in. |
| Muzzle Velocity | 1500 f.s. | Muzzle Velocity | 1150 f.s. | Muzzle Velocity | 1400 f.s. |
| Muzzle Energy | 1049 f.p. | Muzzle Energy | 515 f.p. | Muzzle Energy | 690 f.p. |

# TABLE OF RELATIVE STOPPING POWER AND RECOIL

| | Weight of Bullet (Grains) | Approx. Velocity (Ft. per Second) | Weight of Revolver (Ounces) | Relative Stopping Power | Index Relative Stopping Power .38 Special = 100 | Recoil (Foot Pounds) |
|---|---|---|---|---|---|---|
| .38 Special | 158 | 855 | 32 | 14 | 100 | 3.3 |
| .38 Special Hi Speed | 158 | 1,085 | 31 | 17 | 129 | 5.6 |
| .357 Magnum | 158 | 1,400 | 44 | 28 | 198 | 6.3 |
| .44 Special | 246 | 755 | 36 | 27 | 197 | 5.0 |
| .45 ACP | 246 | 755 | 45 | 27 | 197 | 4.0 |
| .45 Auto Rim | 230 | 805 | 45 | 29 | 214 | 4.3 |
| .45 Colt | 255 | 855 | 47 | 36 | 258 | 5.7 |
| .44 Magnum | 240 | 1,470 | 47 | 64* | 467 | 16.3 |
| .41 Magnum | 210 | 1,500 | 48 | 46 | 332 | 12.5 |
| .41 Magnum | 210 | 1,100 | 48 | 38* | 277 | 6.5 |

*Stopping power values based on Maj. Gen. Julian S. Hatcher's formulas.

†These formulas are approximate, but they do represent the best method presently available for comparison of bullet stopping power.

*Pictured here is the new S&W Model 57 in .41 Magnum caliber. Loads in foreground from left to right: 38 Special and .357 Magnum; .44 Special and .44 Magnum; .41 Magnum lead and jacketed loads.*

Magnum which is a little short on shocking power and the .44 Magnum which has too much; on the back end, anyway. I feel that in time this load will be adopted as a standard by police. That this will not happen overnight is suggested by the .357 Magnum which, after about thirty years, is just becoming so accepted.

I do not intend to write much of this load because I am sure that before this book is printed, reams will have appeared about the "new" .41 Magnum in the gun magazines. However, regarding all the writers who have climbed on the bandwagon and, I am sure, will now make loud claims to have been the pappy or mammy of this load, I wish to make a statement! I tagged along with Elmer Keith and said Amen while Elmer cornered the firearms and ammunition people, individually and collectively, at the 1963 NRA members meeting in Washington and got commitments which actually started the ball to rolling. He badgered Remington and Norma into saying "If someone will make a gun we will make the ammo." . . . Smith and Wesson and Ruger agreed, "We'll make the guns if the ammo people will come up with a load." After that it was just a matter of bringing them together with their commitments, which he did: and a new load was born.

So, regardless of who set the actual dimensions and specifications, it was that grand old man of the shooting game who did the work that made this load a reality. I had hoped that one of the loads would be named the .41 Keith. It would have been fitting recognition to a man who has given much to shooting.

# Practice Loads

WHEN I LOOK back down the years I cannot help but shudder at the memory of thousands of rounds of wadcutter and service loads I have fired in fast-draw point shooting practice. The only defense for this foolishness I can think of quickly is that I did not know of any other way to go about this practice. A more probable answer that occurs to me is that, being young and reckless in those days, I would have probably considered any substitute for the real thing as too sissified for anyone as rough and tough as I fancied myself to be. Be that as it may, from the day I learned about wax bullets I have confined my fast draw practice to the use of that pantywaist gun fodder.

Wax bullet loads consist of all the components of regular ammunition except the powder, with wax being substituted for metal in the projectile. Basically, a de-primed cartridge case is loaded by pushing the mouth through a ½″ cake of paraffin. This cuts out a cylinder of paraffin closely resembling in length, diameter and shape a standard wadcutter bullet for the caliber being loaded. This bullet, of course, is ready "loaded" in the case by the operation of cutting it out. The addition of a fresh primer completes the operation, the piece of paraffin being propelled at considerable velocity and amazing short range accuracy by the explosive force of the primer only. In addition to the obvious advantages of safety, lack of noise, and economy of this loading, is the fact that it can be used for practice with your regular service gun and gives most of the answers with few disadvantages.

Progressing from the basic loading process described above, refinements of technique can add to the quality of the ammunition and increase the production rate far beyond this primitive method. There are presently a number of wax reloading kits on the market, each of which—while basically similar—approach the problem from different angles. Among the better ones of these with which I am familiar are the Pacific Wax Loader, manufactured by Pacific Gunsight Company and the Accra-wax Loader set, put out by the Lyman Gunsight Company. Along with these kits new wax compounds have been developed in an attempt to lessen the disadvantages of plain paraffin. Among these are Accra-wax by Lyman; and the "Red Jet" bullets by Casco Cartridge

Plastic cases and bullets.

Company, in which the material is actually moulded into bullets which are loaded directly into the case mouth with the fingers and may be reused if not fired against a solid object.

Further refinements are exemplified by the use of plastics; both bullets and cases being made from these new materials. These may be purchased from the Speer Products Company of Lewiston, Idaho and from the Plastics Training Products Company of Bloomfield, New Jersey. These plastic bullets may be used over and over and they have further advantages in that they do not melt, nor do they "lead" the barrel as paraffin does. An advantage of the plastic case is that they are so distinctive in appearance that there is no danger of confusing them with "real" ammunition, as is possible when factory brass is reloaded. Additionally, there is a danger inherent in the possible reuse of cases in which the flash holes have been reamed (of which more later), for full charge loads. This is a mistake which the appearance and feel of the plastic cases will preclude.

**84**

Commercial wax loading kits shown are the Lyman Accra Wax and the Pacific. "Red Jet" pre-formed wax bullets in left foreground.

The case holder pictured on right side of picture is machined from a bronze plate. A completely effective simple substitute can be made by cutting off the legs (left) of a plastic cartridge holder from a box of Remington cartridges. Result shown in center.

*Homemade kit. Cake of wax with perforations has already been used and can be discarded or remelted into cake of proper size.*

Although the plastic bullets, new compounds, and commercial loading kits have decided advantages; on the debit side the bullets are considerably more expensive than paraffin, and the "do it yourself" fan can devise a loader which will do a much faster job than anything presently on the market. One such device is illustrated herein. This consists of a metal plate which can be drilled to act as a guide and holder for 50 to 60 .38 Special cases—(the plastic cartridge holder in which Remington .38 Special wadcutters are packed can substitute for this plate by merely cutting off the legs)—and a sturdy wooden or metal box, open on one end, to hold the paraffin and plate in place while pressure is being applied. Its size is predicated on the dimensions of the paraffin cake and the metal plate, both of which should fit snugly within the box. The holes in the plate are filled with de-primed empty cases and placed mouth down on the cake of paraffin within the box. The top is put in place and pushed down with some sort of press. A large vise can be used for this

**86**

purpose, although a bench press is more convenient. As a matter of fact, by first leaving the paraffin block in warm water until it is flexible, the cases may be pressed through merely by the use of hand pressure. The next step, of course, is to remove the "waxed" cases, replace with empties and proceed with your loading.

From the above it will be noted the cases are not primed before "waxing." This is left as a separate operation after the cases have been filled with wax. I have found that when subjected to heat the loads will soften and an oil from the paraffin seeps into the primers and de-activates them. It appears to make little difference to this oil whether the cartridges are stacked base up or base down. It will get to the primers somehow. Accordingly, the cases should be loaded with wax, which is the most time consuming of the loading processes, and the priming left to a convenient time shortly before the loads are to be fired. Of course, the cases are not primed before waxing for the above reason and because, if the primer pocket is sealed, air pressure exerts a piston action, pushing the bullet out of the case.

One difficulty encountered with these squib loads is the tendency of the primer to back out and lock the action. In a regular load, the recoil forces the case head tightly against the face plate of the revolver and thus prevents any backing out of the primer. In wax loads, since there is no recoil and all the force of the explosion occurs in the primer pocket itself, primers which may fit loosely have a tendency to push back. This can be very annoying since often the action will be locked so hard as to require considerable effort to release. It also breaks up any rapid fire sequence. Two remedies are recommended. First, and most effective, ream out the flash hole of each case to a diameter of approximately ⅛ inch. This allows the gas to escape from the primer pocket into the body of the case more quickly, reducing pressures against the primer. Cases so altered should be plainly marked to prevent their reuse with regular powder and lead bullet loads. Pressures would probably be dangerously higher due to the reamed flash hole. An added dividend provided by this operation is a slight increase in velocity. The other remedy is to make certain that primers are fully seated, exerting sufficient pressure in this operation to force them firmly against the bottom of the primer pocket.

Variations in the amount of air space between the base of the wax bullet and the bottom of the case will adversely affect accuracy. To remedy this, push each bullet to the bottom of the case with mild pressure. (Too much pressure would deform the bullet base against the irregular case bottom.) This also expands the nose of the bullet slightly, making it a snugger fit and preventing it

Loading wax bullets using homemade equipment. Paraffin cake placed in bottom of retaining box. De-primed cases loaded into holes drilled through metal block are set mouth down on cake of paraffin.

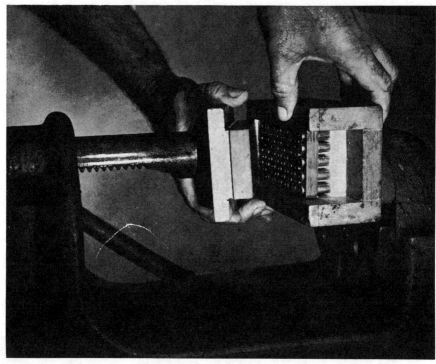

TOP

Box placed in arbor press and fitted wooden block set on top of cases.

Cases being pressed through paraffin cake. Each case acts like miniature "biscuit cutter", cutting out wax "wad cutter" bullets which remain in cases.

After removing from box, turn over and push paraffin bullets to bottom of case. Cases are then removed and after priming, are ready to shoot.

from falling out of the case. This sometimes saves an exhibition shooter considerable embarrassment. Even if *he* is sure the cartridge he just fired was a blank it is a little hard to convince an audience that was the cause of an apparent miss.

Of course it takes all kinds to make a world, so sooner or later you will meet a blood and thunder character who will tell you that he has added considerable tone and quality to his wax bullet loads by the addition of a little black powder. And he will intimate that you should do likewise if you would enjoy all the benefit to be derived from these loads. Actually, this fellow has missed the point entirely. The value of these loads is that they afford accuracy without danger. By increasing the velocity you will lose both advantages. Accuracy is largely due to the spin imparted by the rifling, just as is the case with a metallic bullet. The soft wax cannot stand much velocity without stripping, with the result that it "squirts" out of the barrel with no rotating action. Also, with velocity, it takes on the characteristics of a real bullet and can penetrate to dangerous depth in flesh if fired at close range. The plastic bullets can take more velocity than can the wax, since they are harder and more solid; however, they become even more dangerous. Large pistol primers may be used with the plastic bullets but best results with wax loads are obtained using small primers. Of course, since all the propulsion comes from the primer, it must give consistent pressure if accuracy is to be attained. Of all the primers presently available, the one I have found to be most reliable in this respect is the CCI Magnum primer manufactured by the Cascade Cartridge Company.

The use of wax loads is an invaluable aid to fast draw and hip shooting practice, both for the individual and for departments. As mentioned before, they give the answers without the danger always present with regular loads. They can be fired indoors at moving picture targets where recognition plays a part in training and at a small fraction of the cost of lead and powder loads. One word of caution is worth repetition. Any cartridge cases to be used in this practice should be clearly marked in such a manner as to be highly distinctive. In addition to the already mentioned danger to reloaders, since they are fired in service revolvers, there is always a danger of loading a regular wadcutter in place of the squib load. Use of the plastic cases or properly marking brass cases will reduce the chance of such a mistake to a minimum; however, no possibility should be overlooked and it is a good practice to have the loading checked by a second party before firing is allowed.

# Combat Style Shooting

THE MOST difficult of all firearms to learn to shoot accurately is the handgun. It must be supported by the hands alone at one point, as compared with the rifle where shoulder and hands form a three point support. The sight radius is so short that any error of alignment is magnified tremendously out at the target. This short radius combined with instability of hold make it critically sensitive to any movement caused by pulling the trigger. Originally it was not designed as a precision weapon. Its sole purpose was to be a close range mankiller. In these days of scope sighted handguns chambered for high velocity, super accurate, small caliber cartridges, this purpose has become largely obscured. But the fact remains unchanged. It was designed for self defense at close to medium ranges. It is in this role that the handgun has greatest interest to the lawman.

The only dependable way to learn to shoot a handgun is to start with deliberate, aimed, single action fire at a bull's-eye target until the fundamentals of trigger squeeze and sight alignment are thoroughly mastered. Only then should the shooter concern himself with fast double action shooting. Good habits well learned stay with us for years. Bad habits seem to stay forever. Double action shooting, with its long trigger movement and 15–20 pound pull is infinitely more difficult than single action where a three pound pull will trip the trigger with no perceptible movement. Since the secrets of single action target shooting have been discussed in reams of print, I will write here only of the double action "combat" style, with the comment that the single action fundamentals should be learned first.

Combat shooting, so called, is not confined to any specific style or method. It ranges from fast point-blank hip shooting to single action fire from a rest at long range. Its nature is governed by the situation, with range the greatest single factor in determining the method to be used. Speed is a second limiting factor. There is one common denominator. Its purpose is to get a disabling hit upon an opponent before he can do the same to you, regardless of how you go about it. Style is strictly secondary to effectiveness.

First, let us consider a range of from 0 to 3 yards. At such close distance, which we will call hip shooting range, the shot can be fired at utmost speed and

You would have to be a real old-timer to recognize the hand-
some young fellow under the 40-gallon hat. . . . But if you
don't recognize the HAT. . . . You're just not a gun bug. My
old friend Elmer Keith demonstrates perfect combat shooting
form with two guns

a hit made on a reasonable sized target without the necessity of stopping the gun and consciously bringing it into alignment. The shot can be fired as part of the draw—as soon as the gun clears the holster and is rocked into line. At such close ranges "aiming" is solely by feel. The wrist is relaxed and may be turned for firing in any direction. Accuracy, of course, as at any range, is inversely proportional to the speed with which the shot is fired. If you will pick up a revolver, close your eyes, and wiggle it around you will find that you can actually feel the location of the end of the barrel. This feel is more pronounced with long barrelled guns or with shorter, say 4″, heavy barrels. It is at its weakest with a "snubby," which can be compared to pointing your fist as opposed to pointing your finger. With practice you get this finger pointing feel as soon as you have the weight of the gun in your hand. Accuracy can be extended to seven to ten yards using this method if there is a definite pause for full awareness of the feel, but it is most valuable for those few occasions at close range where you really need to hurry.

From 3 to 7 yards, for want of a better name, let's call it the gun throwing method. Here you must start slowing down as the distance increases. (If you *knew* you had the time, bringing the gun up to eye level would be best at any distance over 5 yards.) This method is similar to an underhand knife toss from level with, and beside the hip. The secret of accuracy is to carry the toss forward against the pull of the muscles in the top of the shoulder until they bring it to a halt. *You should be able to feel full strain against these muscles.* The gun will be very little above belt high and you will be surprised at how smoothly it fires when it hits the end of the line. I believe the reason that this method is so accurate is that swinging the gun forward towards the target gets you in alignment and the pull of the shoulder muscles stopping you at the same time takes care of the elevation problem. Be sure that you reach out to the limit. A try or two will tell you from the feel just what is meant by the above. It is similar to the important trick of aerial shooting, where you must extend your arm as fully as possible toward the target to straighten your elbow. The big difference is that here the elbow is bent and the reaching toward the target is with the shoulder muscles.

From 7 to 15 yards the gun should preferably be held with both hands, particularly if more than one shot is to be fired. It can be fired from belt level at the forward part of this range if speed seems of top importance, but should be brought up fully into the line of sight, even though the sights are not actually used, as the distance increases.

From 15 to 25 yards the gun should be brought up fully into the line of

Left: 0 to 3 yards. Gun barely clears holster as it is rocked into line and fired instantly, with loose wrist by feel of the weapon only. Very fast. For point blank range only.

Left: 3–7 yards. Like tossing a knife underhand. All the way forward against pull of shoulder muscles until these muscles bring arm to a stop.

Right: Closest half of 7–15-yard range. Use both hands, particularly if more than one shot will be fired. A gun fight is not the place to get style conscious!

Right: 15 to 25 yards and beyond. Bring gun further up into line of sight as range increases until sights are being carefully aligned at long ranges.

**95**

Never stand up if you can sit down—and never sit if you can lie down! Colonel Charles Askins demonstrates a combination sitting-prone position. Good for resting and for hitting something at long range. A very practical "sitting" position.

sight. A thing to remember here is that in bringing the gun up you should consciously bring it up *barrel high*. This allows you to get your sights or the barrel aligned more quickly than if the barrel was low so that the front sight is obscured . . . in which case it will have to be tilted into view, the front sight "picked up" and then lowered into the rear notch. A needless waste of time. Firing can be single or double action. At these distances speed *and* accuracy are not likely. At the forward edge of this 15–25 yard boundary, looking down the barrel should be sufficient and faster. As the distance nears the 25 yard mark it is better that you consciously, even though roughly, look through the sights and align them. The gun can either be shot with one hand or held in both. The two handed hold, while of more advantage to the less experienced shooter, won't hurt anybody's shooting, particularly if a series of shots are to be fired.

At over 25 yards shooting should be deliberate, aimed, single action fire, taking advantage of any rest available or holding the gun with both hands for added steadiness. Hits without aiming at 25 yards and beyond, where the strike of the bullet cannot be observed, are mostly accidental.

**96**

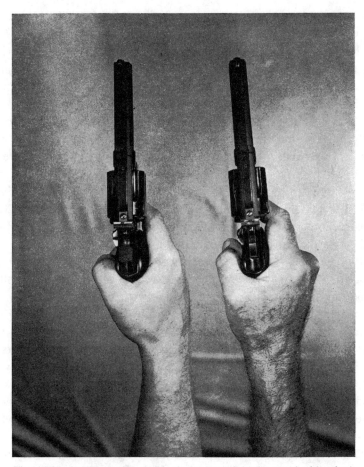

The ideal double action hold shown on right is nearly identical to correct single action grip. Gun is directly in line with forearm. The best that can be done with a small hand shown on left. Necessary to reach around to reach trigger.

In any of the above methods of firing, the one most important item is, of course, trigger control. Particularly in double action fire great care must be taken to exert straight back pressure smoothly with the trigger finger only. Pressure on one side of the trigger or squeezing with all the fingers will make the gun move on let-off and you will have a miss. This is necessary even when "digging out." You must control the trigger. In this connection there are two schools of thought as to the best system of double action trigger control. One of these theories is that the trigger should be brought quickly back to a point just short of firing and then deliberately squeezed off from that point. In the other system the trigger is pulled straight through without hesitation. Personally, although I have seen fine shooting done using the first method, I favor the second style for the following reasons: The system of a two stage pull appears to me to have no appreciable speed advantage over single action fire, inasmuch as a trained shooter can cock a revolver about as fast as the hammer can be moved back by the double action method, if the double action shooter is concentrating on stopping that movement before the gun fires; it is not as accurate as single action; and there is always a possibility of firing before ready due to going past the stopping point. Additionally, I think that a person would be more apt to flinch under the pressure of a gun fight if using this method. The straight through pull is much faster and more positive. Due to the construction of the weapons, a Colt lends itself admirably to the two stage method while the S&W is the better for a one stage pull.

Another question which is often asked concerns the correct hand and trigger finger position for double action shooting. Needless to say, the best position is the same one used in single action fire, with the exception that the thumb should not ride high but should be curled firmly down onto the second finger. The revolver should be a continuation of the straight line of the forearm and the trigger should be contacted at a point midway between the tip and first joint of the index finger. This is the *best* position, but unfortunately we are restricted in these matters by the size, shape, and strength of the hands. Very few people have sufficient power in the trigger finger to use the position described above to deliver a smooth double action pull. Most are compelled to place the second joint on the trigger in order to pull it smoothly. This, unless the hand is very large and the finger unusually long, requires that a grip much further around to the right than is desirable be taken in order to properly position the finger. If you have the hands for it, use the orthodox grip and pull. If you don't, improvise the best possible grip that will allow you to make a smooth, straight back pull on the trigger. Remember—the trigger pull is the important item—not the grip. As a matter of fact, when drawing and firing quickly, one is seldom skillful or lucky enough to get a perfect grip—which matters very little if the trigger is properly controlled. Practice, of course, is the ultimate secret. For distances up to 7 yards, wax bullet loads should be used. They give you the answers without any of the danger of fast work with live ammo.

One last suggestion: For 90% of your practice, draw from the holster and fire one shot. It's that first shot that is important and it is the one most difficult to place accurately. *Don't* practice "hosing" your shots, depending on seeing hits to get you on target. You learn nothing from this and you are lost if you can't see the strike of your bullets. Your crutch won't work at night or with no background to mark your shots, and then you will be in bad trouble. The first shot is all important, and if it is in, the others will follow.

For the other 10%, if you are concentrating on that first shot and it goes in you will have no difficulty with the rest of the burst. Your wrist and forearm will stiffen automatically for recoil control. And above all, take all the time necessary but don't dawdle. Remember, "speed's fine, but accuracy's final"—if you are given time to display it!

# Gun Fighting

SEVERAL YEARS ago Harlon Carter, later Chief of the U. S. Border Patrol and now a Regional Commissioner of the Immigration Service, was glumly reviewing scores fired by himself in a Florida Pistol Match in which he had finished in second place, only a few points behind Harry Reeves. This untoward finish was the result of a mental lapse accompanied by a twitch of the right index finger about halfway through the .45 Rapid Fire Match, which same had cost him a whole fistful of points and untold mental anguish. So Mr. Carter was engaged in the popular pastime known to pistol shooters and poker players the world over as "rabbit hunting." In retrospect, he had just refired that fateful rapid fire string and was going into the .45 National Match Course (which he had won handily—and actually) two points ahead of the eventual winner. It was at this unfortunate moment that he was approached by a well meaning individual and congratulated on his fine performance. Carter's face turned a choleric red and his neck swelled a full inch to a size nineteen, but with admirable restraint, before stalking stiff-legged away, he merely remarked with great dignity: "I wouldn't wish my worst enemy second place"!!!!!

The repressed bitterness behind that statement is known only too well to match shooters. The winner of each class gets a trophy, assorted merchandise prizes and the plaudits of the populace. The runner-up has to be content with a second place medal and the knowledge that within a week no one will know *who* was second in the match, nor care. He is a sad *hombre,* but his unhappy plight can well be envied by the man who comes out second in a pistol duel. Not even a medal for him. The only prize he's likely to get is a monument. THERE IS NO SECOND PLACE WINNER IN A GUN FIGHT!!!!!

That sage remark is of unrivaled importance to an enforcement officer. Nothing he can buy from a life insurance firm takes the place of his ability to shoot fast and accurately. Storebought insurance will make his wife a rich widow, but it will be someone else who helps her spend the settlement. Not too attractive a proposition from the masculine point of view. The kind of life insurance he can buy with competent gun handling ability is obviously much more practical.

No normal man likes the thought of using a lethal weapon upon another

These are excellent side views of a correct double action grip. Note the thumb folded down against fingers. Although the trigger has already gone forward, the bottom figure was taken as a contrast shot at top of recoil, .44 Magnum fired from the hip. Note the very slight upward movement as compared with top photo taken just before firing and that there has been no movement of the weapon in the hand. This last is due to a good grip and well designed grips.

human. However, just as there are countries who have no regard for the rights of other countries and use force to take what rightfully belongs to those other countries, we have individuals who operate on the same brutal principle. Both are criminals and both must be dealt with. To protect us from such countries we have our armed forces. Law enforcement officers perform this duty on an individual basis. In either case, superior force is the only thing that criminals fully understand.

Many thousands of words have been written about "combat" shooting. Unfortunately, the subject as usually handled is a misnomer. What is really described at such length is a game. The equipment and methods described are suited for competition with firearms under conditions which *might* occur in an actual gunfight, but seldom do. I have no quarrel with such games, even though the seriousness with which they are treated in print is often amusing. They are just as good as any other shooting game and more practical than most. They at least give some practice in a part of gunfighting which can be practiced: double action shooting under tightly restricted time limits. They certainly have more practical features than either our National Match Course or, the other extreme, fast draw blank popping. However, the fact remains that these all are games and should be considered as such. Otherwise, some basically wrong thinking, particularly as to equipment, can result.

In this connection the question can be raised "What is real combat equipment?" I have read recent articles in which the author had very definite ideas on the subject. They were good ideas, but they were not on the subject he thought he was covering. The designs of leather and the weapons advocated were combat *competition* rigs. The automatics favored were fine for competition but impractical for everyday usage, *as altered*. They also were sadly lacking in stopping power. The holsters slanted back and in some models were strapped to the leg. Designs that might be excellent if an officer's career was going to be one big continuous battle, but uncomfortable and impractical for everyday use.

By now the answer to the question posed above must be quite obvious. Real combat equipment is that gun and holster you carry forty hours a week plus overtime. That's the one you are going to be wearing when trouble starts. You can't figure on one rig for peace and one for war. If you can, make that war rig a sawed-off shotgun and quit bothering about unimportant details!

In this book the fundamentals of the types of shooting most likely to be useful in combat and the fundamentals of fast draw have been treated at some length. Study of these and other articles can form a basis on which an officer can prepare himself for combat situations, but from this point a literary hiatus is encountered. If anything instructive has been written on the subject of gunfighting, not as a game but as a grim reality, it has remained obscure. There are probably several reasons for this omission: among them a natural reluctance to write of the particulars of such a bloody business, aggravated by a ridiculous taboo against any suggestion in writing that a handgun might be used for another purpose than punching neat holes in a paper target. A more likely reason for this dearth of material on the subject is that combat has no rules and no clear-cut pattern which can be reduced to essentials and set up in a training formula. There is no manual for gunfighting! It is different from military warfare where, in even guerilla fighting, there is a set objective of capturing or clearing territory. The only objectives in gunfighting are to live and either capture or kill your opponent. You learn by experience—assuming survival. Each fight is different and the officer must react differently—and always correctly—to each. These reactions, even if proven correct by their success, are not always logical appearing. At times the right action is "sensed" against all logic and the wise man follows his hunch and lives. Instinct, born of a terrible desire to survive, takes over; perceptions are sharpened and the right move is taken because of subconscious reactions; the result of these abnormally sharpened perceptions.

Feeling the need of some guidelines of survival in gunfighting, but realizing that no hard and fast rules can apply, this section of this book will be devoted to a discussion of a few "tricks of the trade." Just as there is little continuity in a gun fight, there will be little here. Disjointed bits of information will make up most of this treatment. In writing this chapter I do not wish to create the impression that I am claiming to be an authority on the subject, or that the coverage given is complete. On the other hand, no apologies are believed to be in order. The information presented, while neither new nor startling, has been passed around campfires and over coffee tables by fighting men the world over, and is for the most part completely simple and obvious. In the belief that sometimes the simplest and most obvious features are least observed, these "tips" are herewith presented. Most of these comments, while descriptive of outdoor situations, apply equally to city conditions. A bullet doesn't know the difference between a rock and a fire plug. The back yards, alleys and tenements of a city are a jungle where a mistake is just as final as it would be on a brush lined bank of the Rio Grande.

A competitor in a pistol match, conventional or combat style, would be thrown off the line for unsportsmanlike conduct if he tried to take an unfair

**104**

advantage to himself. We would all feel that his actions were deplorable, and that his punishment was justified. This is an attitude which must be quickly and firmly suppressed in mental conditioning for combat. Here is a game in which you cannot afford to be a good loser—or any other kind. In a gunfight you must take every advantage possible. Advantages which *can* be taken will make up most of this article.

Any competitive pistol shooter will tell you that the most difficult action under the stress of competition is to exert a smooth, even pull on the trigger. This is a result of nervous tension, caused mostly by a desire to make a good showing before the public. Consider, if you will, how this pressure is intensified under combat conditions. The desire to appear well is replaced by a much stronger desire just to continue to appear! You are struck with the realization that your opposition is a man who is trying to kill you and that in the next instant the world may have to find someone else to revolve about. His bullet may end life for you! Nothing in your prior experience, except gunfighting, can prepare you for this shocking thought. At this point the steadiness of the target range is liable to desert you and you may tend to discard all the fundamentals in a desperate attempt to get your shot in first. Here is where training takes over or you break up.

A question often asked of themselves by young officers is, "How will I comport myself in the face of fire? Will I stand up or will I break?" On the surface this would appear to be a question which can be answered only if it becomes an actuality. As a matter of fact the answer can be given with very little chance of error. Almost invariably a man, provided he does not have too much time to think, will automatically do what he has been trained to do. Again provided that his training has been thorough and intensive. An example in support of this statement comes to my mind: A few years back a Border Patrol team became involved in a discussion with some *contrabandistas* in which they were considerably embarrassed by one of the smugglers holed up in some brush about 200 yards away. His presence unduly complicated the proceedings in that he was armed with a .30–30 rifle with which he was enthusiastically underscoring points in the argument made by the main group of his compatriots. The Border Patrolmen were armed only with .38 Special revolvers which put them at somewhat of a disadvantage under the circumstances. However, two of the three men applied themselves to the task of routing the nearby enemy while the senior officer, Sam McKone, took up the question of the rifleman in the brush.

They tell of a western epitaph which reads, "Here lies Tom Jones. Committed suicide by betting his pistol against a rifle at 200 yards." This could be a normal result of such a contest, but Sam McKone is not one of the Jones boys. Among his other marksmanship awards is a gold medal declaring him to be a Distinguished Pistol Shot. Additionally, being shot at was not a matter to distress Sam unduly, since it was not exactly a novel occurrence in his life. To make a long story short, by applying a little Kentucky windage and an educated trigger squeeze, Sam scored three hits which made the rifle shooter lose all interest in the fate of his companions and start thinking solely of his own welfare, here and hereafter. What has all this to do with the statement that a man will do unconsciously as he was trained, provided the training was thorough and extensive? Well, after the fight someone noted that McKone's pocket was bulging and politely inquired as to what might be spoiling the drape of his trousers. Puzzled, Sam thrust in an exploring hand. The pocket was full of fired cases. During the fight, without realizing he was doing so, McKone, an old reloader, had saved every empty!

It has been previously mentioned that nervous tension makes it difficult to squeeze a trigger smoothly. This is further complicated in a gunfight by a natural disinclination to pull the trigger at all when your weapon is pointed at a human. Even though their own life was at stake, most officers report having this trouble in their first fight. To aid in overcoming this reluctance it is helpful if you can will yourself to think of your opponent as a mere target and not as a human being. In this connection you should go further and pick a spot on the target. This will allow better concentration and further remove the human element from your thinking. If this works for you, try to continue this thought that you were shooting a target after the fight is over. There is no point in allowing yourself to feel remorse. A man who will resist an officer with weapons has no respect for the rules by which decent people are governed. He is an outlaw who has no place in world society. His removal is completely justified, and should be accomplished dispassionately and without regret.

I consider myself fortunate in having known one of the greatest peace officers this country has produced—Captain John Hughes of the Texas Rangers. I met him through his close friendship with my late uncle, Dr. Ira Bush of El Paso. Dr. Bush, I might mention in passing, was surgeon-general of the Insurrecto Army under General Madero and Pancho Villa and wrote a book of his experiences called *Gringo Doctor*. At the time I knew Captain Hughes I was a young man just starting in law enforcement, while he was quite elderly and long retired from active service. Like most old timers, he was reluctant to talk of personal experiences but occasionally passed out advice well worth heeding. One such gem that I have always remembered and will pass on was: "If you get in a gunfight, don't let yourself feel rushed. Take your time, fast."

Now this is advice not easy to follow when you are being shot at and constantly reminded by the whine of bullets that man, meaning you, is mortal. But all the knowledge you will ever learn about gun fighting is summed up in those words. When you *really understand* their full meaning, you have come of age. In order to follow this advice, mental discipline, the result of previous hard thinking, is a must. And here a little applied psychology pays off. You must force yourself to the belief that your opponent is going to choke up and miss and that all you have to do to win is keep cool and make your shot—the first one—a hit. This without letting your manufactured contempt get out of hand and cause you to take foolish chances! With the vast majority of us this attitude must be forced. In an occasional rare individual it is natural. He responds to danger by turning into a machine—ignoring the fire of his opponents and placing his shots as though indulging in private target practice. This is your true gun fighter. Of such material were the John Wesley Hardins and other big names of a bygone era made.

Your movie-TV type of gunfight where two men stalked grimly toward each other down a dusty street seldom if ever happened. Most of the battles between officers and criminals have taken place under conditions of close range and poor light and have borne little resemblance to the traditional personal duel. Usually, several men were involved and they had plenty of advance warning to enable them to fight from cover with weapons ready and opponents chosen haphazardly as targets of opportunity. Occasionally, however, a man-to-man situation evolves out of the big picture where a man is required to literally beat his opponent to the draw. This can come about in a number of ways, none of them often planned in advance! Usually in such cases both men will react spontaneously, going for their guns, if not already drawn, and shooting as quickly as possible. If this should occur at extreme close range—powder burning distance—speed is of the essence. The man firing first will probably win—unless he gets in *too* big a hurry and fires before he finishes drawing. It is well for *you* to realize that there is a natural inclination to fire before the gun is level. The answer to that problem is to *think* that you will get a high let-off. Your shot will probably go off about navel height if you are thinking strongly of a high chest or throat hit. In a situation such as the above where you are not close enough to get a sure hit with the gun moving in the motion of drawing, "Take your time, fast" applies. Pick the biggest, easiest and softest target—the middle—and make your first shot good. The amount of time you take, and how fast you take it, will depend almost entirely on the distance of your target. Before hostilities are opened, never make a threatening motion without carrying it through. It may trigger your opponent's reflexes and you will find yourself left at the gate. On the other hand, even if he starts first, there is a good chance that *he* will hesitate. You keep a-coming and maybe you can take advantage of that hesitation and catch up enough to get there first. It doesn't pay to give up.

A gunfight is not a sporting event. Rules of fair play do not apply. If there is any advantage to be had, be sure that your side takes it. More often than not, the officers will know that an arrest is to be made and will have a good idea whether the man or men to be arrested will be resentful to a positive degree. Here a little advance planning is indicated. If possible, choose the battleground and choose it with an eye to giving yourself all the breaks. You should pick a position where any dazzling light will be to your back and in their eyes. But be sure that you are not skylighted and that your background and clothing blend. If your partner is one of long standing, each of you will probably know how the other will react. In any event, prearranged plans and signals for action should be set up and clearly understood. By all means, be sure that your positions will complement each other so as to deliver the heaviest and most effective fire on your opponents. There should be no possibility of a maneuver on their part which could put you in your partner's line of fire or vice versa. Of course, any or all of the above measures may be impossible. Just be sure that you don't miss one that is possible.

Any element of surprise can be used in your favor. If you are in the presence of a man you intend to arrest, watch him carefully. If he puts himself in a bad position such as sitting in a chair with arms, which would impede his access to a weapon, take instant advantage of any such mistake on his part and take him then. On the contrary, if either of his hands are out of sight the practice of patience would be advisable. Those hidden hands could be holding aces.

Don't let your face or eyes give away your intention. If you can't depend on a dead pan poker face remaining that way, smile! Then make your move and *carry it all the way through*. If force is required, use enough to do the job, use it first and without hesitation.

In arresting a man you have reason to believe to be dangerous, never give an order such as the traditional "hands up" which would lead you to *expect* his hands to move and might give him a winning start over your reflexes. The

**108**

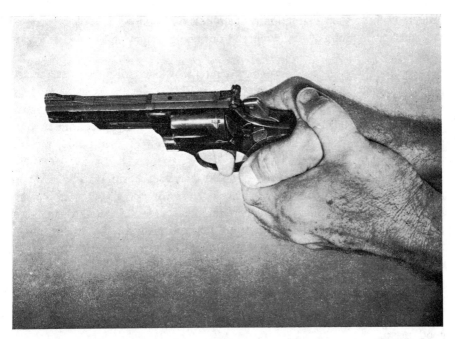

Good two handed grips shown above and below. Using grip at top, left thumb is used for cocking to fire single action.

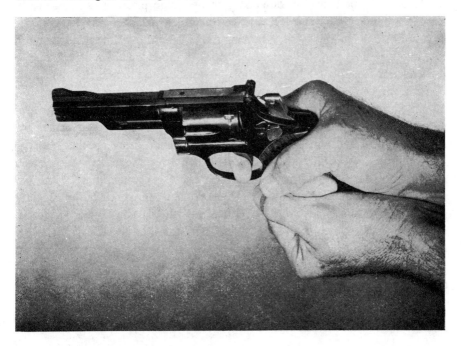

prudent order in such a situation is "Don't move!" Followed by observance of the usual precautions of searching and disarming taught any rookie at police school.

If you should be engaged at night or the target is otherwise poorly defined so that you cannot be sure of a hit, hold low. The tendency is to shoot high anyway and while a shot too high is of no value, a low shot might give you a richochet hit. Besides, even if a miss, it will be more disconcerting to your opponents hitting the ground where it can be seen or heard than moving undetected through the air.

In a predicament where to move would give your position away, such as might be the case in a dark room or alley where you know your man is near, but neither of you knows exactly where the other is, sometimes throwing your hat or some other object will draw his fire and give you an aiming point. Speaking of hats: throwing yours into the face of a man with the "drop" could distract him enough to give you your chance.

Now for a few don'ts:

Be sure that you have correctly identified your target, then *lock on* and keep with it. Don't switch as long as your original target is available without a very good reason.

Unless you are directly engaged in a close range brawl where movement would draw immediate fire, don't stay in the same place after firing. Keep moving around. This can keep your opponent off balance—maybe guessing at your position. In any event, a moving target is harder to hit even if you are caught out in the open. It is *generally* better to move toward your left due to the tendency most people have to "milk" their shots to the left. But remember that this can be made to work two ways. Try shooting slightly to your right of his gun flash at night instead of directly at it. (If he's left handed, you are real unlucky!) And if you think he is firing and moving, a shot placed well to the right just might find him at home . . . which should bring another message home to you . . . while profiting by any such error by an opponent, avoid setting a predictable pattern of your own.

In using a flashlight don't hold it in front of you when you turn it on. Hold it at arm's length to the side. Remember that a flashlight allows you to see but also makes a target of you, so use it sparingly. Flash it on to pick up the target and then turn it off—unless you know that you have only one man to deal with and you can flash it in his eyes. If you should be so lucky, hold it there and make your move. You couldn't ask for better odds than that!

Don't wear light colored clothing, particularly at night. And above all, don't

**110**

wear a white shirt. It makes a beautiful bull's-eye. And if hit is very little protection to the vitals it so conveniently pinpoints for the opposition.

Don't stand in the open. Use any cover available; and let's differentiate between cover and concealment. Crouching behind a wooden barrel would give you concealment, but very little protection from a bullet. Now if that barrel was full of water you would have both—although it would be a good idea to have some place else picked to go, in case your barrel sprang a leak! Just being hidden is not enough, but it beats being out in the open. And remember—shoot around the side of cover, not over the top. If no cover is available, hit the deck. Don't mind the mud or filth, it will wash off. Just get down there and make the smallest target possible—and for good measure, fire, then *roll* to make yourself even more difficult to hit.

The old adage, "Don't draw unless you *intend* to shoot" is poor advice. It should read, "Don't draw unless you are *ready* to shoot." Pulling a gun in a situation where its use is not justified can wind up as highly embarrassing, particularly if there are witnesses and the subject, sensing his advantage, should pull some such histrionics as baring his chest and daring the officer to shoot! On the other hand, there's no gainsaying the fact that "the fastest draw is to have the gun in your hand when the fight starts," provided you are ready to use it if necessary. It is an almost unbelievable fact that every year officers are killed entering a *known* dangerous situation with holstered gun when they might have lived had they taken the precaution of drawing the weapon before the situation developed.

Don't use your gun as a club. There are seldom occasions when use of a club is required to subdue a prisoner or to defend yourself. If the situation has gotten that far out of control, use of the gun for the purpose for which it was designed will likely be in order. And, in establishing the "amount of force which was necessary," you will probably find it easier to convince a coroner's jury that you didn't shoot him too much than that you didn't hit him too hard. Besides which, a gun makes a very poor bludgeon. Due to the sharp corners, while it will cut the scalp and probably cave in sections of bone, it seldom stuns the person hit as would a smooth, blunt object. If other arguments against this practice are needed, the following may be considered: A swing and a near miss, such as might allow the wrist to hit instead of the gun, will probably cause the gun to be dropped, leaving the officer unarmed; and, all handguns have vulnerable points where a relatively light blow can cause a part to be bent, jamming the action and making the weapon inoperative.

And one more thing: Pure "guts" have won many a gun fight. The man who has enough determination is hard to down. You can keep on fighting even if you are hit. If you make up your mind that you are going to get your bullet into the other man, you will probably do it. And maybe that hit you took will turn out not so bad as you thought, particularly if you stop him and keep him from hitting you again. Doctors will tell you that many men give up and die from wounds which were superficial, or which in any event should not have been fatal. So don't forget—with enough determination you can win even when you appear to be losing—just keep shooting!

# Summation

HUNDREDS OF articles have been written by highly competent authors on the basic fundamentals of shooting. A description of the individual steps which make up good marksmanship: holding, sight alignment, trigger squeeze; are available in books, pamphlets and magazine articles readily available to any interested person. Similarly, a beginning officer has at his disposal the fundamentals of his profession spelled out in laws and statutes and amplified by the writings of experts. He is taught his duties and authorities in enforcing the law in police schools and academies.

If it appears to the reader that I have ignored these fundamentals in this book, his impression is only partially true. Let us say instead that I have intentionally failed to cover these points in the belief that what has already been well done many times over should not be belaboured here. In describing basic methods of combat shooting I have mentioned that I considered this type of gun work in the nature of postgraduate study, which should be attempted *only* after the shooter was well grounded in all the details which make up good, deliberate, aimed, single action marksmanship. Likewise, if I have failed to point out in the chapter on gun fighting the limitations set on the use of firearms by an officer in the performance of his duty, it is not due to lack of awareness or concern with these matters, but because I feel that these limitations have been too well defined elsewhere to give value to further mention here.

What I have tried to do instead, is to enter a field of professional marksmanship on which very little has been written by competent authorities and to describe equipment, its care and use, in a way seldom, if ever, to be found in a textbook or offered in formal training courses.

I realize that very few pages have been used to cover a subject on which many pages could be written. This brevity has been deliberate. It was my wish to present a text in which the grain could be harvested without too much winnowing of the chaff. I have tried to write in such a way that there could be no misunderstanding of my meanings and so that reference could be made to any subject covered without undue search through a rubble of unnecessary verbiage.

It was my thought that putting these matters down in print might be of great aid to young officers, and as I laboured over these pages I was warmed by a feeling of good doing and conscious worth . . . now that I have finished, some doubt intrudes. Looking back down the years of my own career, I do not recall many instances when I heeded the advice of my elders, preferring, as do most young men, to learn by my own mistakes. This system has always worked very well, since scars and bruises serve to underline a lesson learned. The only trouble with this trial and error method, as regards the training of an officer, is the inordinate amount of good luck sometimes required to complete the course.

To persons leading more sedentary lives who chance to read these words, a small glimpse into the lives of the men who stand watch while you sleep should have been afforded. It is my hope that you have been in some measure entertained and at the same time given more understanding of their problems and more tolerance of their actions.

To the lawman of the future: I believe that the principles discussed herein will be of meaning in your time. Not as historic data but as a living text to aid officers in carrying out their duties in the world to come. Man has traveled far . . . but I do not foresee a time when his combative, covetous nature will not cause the less restrained to run afoul of constituted authority. So . . . although the weapons of tomorrow may become more sophisticated and the locale may be literally out of this world, I have confidence that the lawman's ancient adversary will still be in operation—and that he will still resent the placing of a curb on his larcenous or murderous impulses to a positive degree. In which case . . . maybe this book will help you. Good hunting.

# NOTES

# NOTES

# NOTES

# NOTES

# NOTES

# NOTES

# NOTES

# NOTES

# NOTES

# NOTES